The Limits of Alliance

THE NEW INTERNATIONAL RELATIONS OF EUROPE
Series Editor: Ronald H. Linden

The Limits of Alliance

The United States, NATO, and the EU in North and Central Europe

Andrew A. Michta

ROWMAN & LITTLEFIELD PUBLISHERS, INC.
Lanham · Boulder · New York · Toronto · Oxford

ROWMAN & LITTLEFIELD PUBLISHERS, INC.

Published in the United States of America
by Rowman & Littlefield Publishers, Inc.
A wholly owned subsidiary of The Rowman & Littlefield Publishing Group, Inc.
4501 Forbes Boulevard, Suite 200, Lanham, Maryland 20706
www.rowmanlittlefield.com

P.O. Box 317, Oxford OX2 9RU, UK

British Library Cataloguing in Publication Information Available

Library of Congress Cataloging-in-Publication Data
Michta, Andrew A.
   The limits of alliance : the United States, NATO, and the EU in North and Central
Europe / Andrew A. Michta.
       p. cm. — (The new international relations of Europe)
   Includes bibliographical references and index.
   ISBN-13: 978-0-7425-3864-1 (cloth : alk. paper)
   ISBN-10: 0-7425-3864-8 (cloth : alk. paper)
   ISBN-13: 978-0-7425-3865-8 (pbk. : alk. paper)
   ISBN-10: 0-7425-3865-6 (pbk. : alk. paper)
   1. Europe—Foreign relations—1989. 2. European Union countries—Foreign relations.
3. North Atlantic Treaty Organization. 4. National security—Europe. 5. Europe—
Foreign relations—United States. 6. United States—Foreign relations—Europe. I.
Title. II. Series.

D2003.M53 2006
327.730409'0511—dc22   2005035307

Printed in the United States of America

⊚™ The paper used in this publication meets the minimum requirements of
American National Standard for Information Sciences—Permanence of Paper
for Printed Library Materials, ANSI/NISO Z39.48-1992.

To Cristina and Chelsea

Contents

Acknowledgments

$\mathscr{T}$his project has been in the making for the past four years, morphing as rapid changes in international security have redefined its scope and focus. I wish to extend my special thanks to Col. Tim Park, Titt Noorkoiv, Trivimi Velliste, Tom Ilves, Mari-Ann Kelam, Edgars Rinkevis, Ojars Kalnins, Atis Lejins, Evaldal Ignatavicius, Kestutis Jankauskas, Gen. Jonas Kronkaitis, Graham Roberts, Col. Romas Petkevicius, Linas Linkevicius, Algirdas Gricius, Dick Krickus, Tapani Vaahtoranta, Elina Kalkku, Raimo Väyrynen, Olli Kivinen, Michael Borg-Hansen, Tomas Ries, Michael Ehrenreich, Jens-Otto Horslund, Thomas Ostrup Moller, Ann-Sophie Dahl, Per Carlsen, Bertel Heurlin, Mikael Holmstrom, Bo Hugemark, Henrik Landerholm, Henrik Landerholm, Ingemar Dorfer, Pär Eriksson, Niclas Trouvé, Gen. Michael Moore, Catharina Wale-Grunditz, Gen. Jan-Gunnar Isberg, Katarina Engberg, Karlis Neretnieks, Robert Dalsjö, Anette Nielsson, Jørg Willy Bronebakk, Ole Terje Horpestad, Bård Bredrup Knudsen, Olav Riste, Klaus Becher, Detlef Puhl, Lord William Wallace, Edward Foster, Mats Berdal, Gen. Sir Jeremy Mackenzie, Malcolm Haworth, John Lough, Anthony Forester, Chris Donnelly, Neil Grayston, Col. Leszek Soczewica, Gen. Edward Pietrzyk, Gen. Franciszek Gągor, Sean Kay, Jeff Simon, and Josh Spero for their help in my research.

I wish to thank the Woodrow Wilson Center for its generous support during my residence as Public Policy Scholar when the first draft of this book was completed. I am especially grateful to Martin Sletzinger, Director of East European Studies at the Wilson Center, and to his assistants Meredith Knepp and Sabina Crisen for their friendship and encouragement. I also wish to thank the Institute for European, Russian and Eurasian Studies of the George Washington University for welcoming me as its Research Associate and for its continued support of my work. A word of thanks goes to the Hoover Institution, especially its tireless library staff, Linda Wheeler, Molly Molloy, and Maria Quinonez, for their hospitality and assistance. Special thanks go to the Series Editor Ronald Linden for his friendship and support, which made this book possible. I also wish to thank Robert Buckman for his friendship and continued support of my research.

This book has benefited from comments and advice from a great number of people in government, academia, and the policy community in the United States and in Europe. They are too numerous to name here, but to all of them I owe my sincere word of thanks. I am truly indebted to Lynn Keathley, my research assistant, whose perseverance and hard work were matched only by her good cheer throughout this project. And very special thanks go to my wife Cristina and my daughter Chelsea for their love and their patience.

Introduction

WHEN ALLIANCES FADE

In the past decade academic scholarship has accorded the issue of regional security in northern and central Europe limited attention. That is mainly because the region's benign security environment has been in sharp contrast to the situation in other parts of the world. The region's stability has strengthened the view that, between the disintegration of the Soviet Union in 1991 and the dual enlargement of the North Atlantic Treaty Organization (NATO) and the European Union (EU) in 2004, the countries of northern and central Europe have completed their post–Cold War transformation. Extension into the region of the overlapping institutional frameworks of NATO and the EU is often seen as the final step in that process. Notwithstanding the impressive record of the past decade, including the integration of the postcommunist states into the transatlantic security system, the region's geostrategic position as Europe's eastern boundary makes its security an ongoing concern.

This is a book about changes in the security of northern and central Europe, set against a slowly unraveling NATO, the nascent but insufficiently cohesive European Security and Defense Policy (ESDP),[1] and the post–September 11, 2001, American Global War on Terrorism (GWOT), as the United States continues to seek a strategy that will bridge the transatlantic fissures opened in the run-up to the Second Iraq War, which began in 2003. Its goal is not to analyze in great detail the internal dynamics of devolving NATO and the evolving ESDP, both of which have been covered in a number of recent publications, nor is it to propose how the United States ought to pursue its campaign against jihadi terrorism. Rather, the book intends to contribute to the debate on the state of transatlantic relations by looking at where

1

North and Central Europe fit in the post–September 11 security dynamic, especially in the context of NATO's ongoing transformation. It is an insight into how northern and central Europeans have adapted their national security policies at a time when traditional alliances can be seen as wanting.

At another level, the book concerns the need to rethink the residual assumptions about the future of alignments inherited from the Cold War era. Accordingly, it will survey the security policies of the states in North and Central Europe in order to highlight how historical legacies, regional geostrategic constraints, and individual military capabilities have shaped their response to the new environment. It will argue that although in the coming decade NATO will continue to exist, a sub rosa shift is under way in transatlantic security relations, toward U.S.–state bilateralism determined by regional security considerations, with the central question whether the EU as a unitary actor can become and be accepted as a partner for the United States.

This book seeks to outline the limits of residual Cold War alignments in the post–September 11 world. It raises the larger question of whether NATO and alliances in general are an optimum vehicle for dealing with the new security environment. In the world of post-Westphalian terrorist threats generated by substate actors, alliances are likely to see their utility dwindle further. In the era of international terrorism and religiously defined conflict, traditional state-to-state alignments may prove to be at best tangential to the threats confronting democratic governments today.

Historically, alliances have been formed in response to state-level threats. It is not surprising that the core ideas of transatlantic solidarity that undergirded Western security during and after the Cold War have with each passing year become less and less germane to the realities of twenty-first-century global security. That trend had become increasingly apparent even before the shock of the September 11, 2001, terrorist attacks on the World Trade Center and the Pentagon. In the wake of the demise of the Warsaw Pact and the attendant loss of NATO's central purpose, the alliance began to show signs of institutional malaise, finding it progressively more difficult to move beyond the political decisions on enlargement and push the new as well as the old allies in the direction of meaningful military modernization. The gradual decline of NATO had its roots in the global geostrategic shift caused by the end of the Cold War, but the dynamic of the two cycles of institutional enlargement and the operations in the Balkans, including NATO's military campaign in Kosovo and its aftermath, were also contributing factors. By the time the second cycle of enlargement came in 2004, NATO found itself all but overpowered by major differences of view among its key players and strained by the bureaucratic demands of enlargement. The alliance was increasingly losing its primary focus on its military mission. In the 1990s the allies were reluctant to ask the hard questions about NATO's future as a military organization, even as NATO debated the political implications of bringing in new members. NATO's Cold War task of collective defense against the Warsaw Pact belonged in the history books, but there was little agreement on the nature of emerging threats and the requisite investment in defense capabilities to counter them. Even after NATO's 1999 air campaign against Serbia there was no clear consensus as to whether the Kosovo operation marked NATO's decisive step toward "out-of-area" operations or the campaign should be viewed as an exception.

Following the 2004 enlargement, NATO faced the task of absorbing seven new entrants that, for all practical purposes, offered only marginal military value. With the possible exceptions of Romania and Bulgaria, which provided territory and bases useful for U.S. operations in Central Asia and the Middle East, most of the new NATO members brought negligible assets to the alliance, arguably supplying even less value than the 1999 Central European trench did. One could credibly argue in 1999 that NATO's enlargement into Poland, Hungary, and the Czech Republic had not only addressed an important geostrategic imperative by stabilizing the periphery of united Germany but in the process had brought in one potentially meaningful military contributor—Poland. One would be hard-pressed, however, to assert anything comparable about the potential military contributions of the 2004 trench. All of the countries included in the 2004 NATO enlargement were small states with limited power potential. The combined populations of Latvia, Lithuania, and Estonia (the three Baltic States), plus the populations of Slovenia and Slovakia, total well below 15 million, but the new allies account for seven votes in the North Atlantic Council (NAC), the organization's highest policy and decision-making body, and expand NATO's defense obligations into some of Europe's historically most sensitive areas: the Balkans, northeastern Europe, and the Baltic littoral. Had NATO's commitment to those important geopolitical regions been accompanied by a new consensus on mission and capabilities, the 2004 enlargement could have revitalized NATO; its absence underscored how far the alliance had devolved into a political organization.

Arguably, the most important question for the future of transatlantic relations that this book addresses is whether NATO still matters to the United States beyond immediate political utility. There is no question that since the United States and a number of Continental states have parted ways on Iraq and critical issues of Middle East security, Washington can look to the residual institutional framework of the NATO alliance as a vehicle for political support and a source of potential participants in "coalitions of the willing."[2] Unless NATO restores a general sense of shared mission and military planning relevant to new threats, however, it is unlikely in the coming years to recover its institutional cohesion and ability to act collectively.

NATO had been struggling with the questions of security identity and mission for more than a decade prior to the events of September 11, 2001, long before the rupture in transatlantic relations in March 2003 over the U.S. decision to go to war against Iraq became apparent, but the September 11 attacks and American strategy in the war against jihadi terrorism accelerated NATO's decline. Since September 11, the United States and Europe have been searching for an alternative to the decomposing post–Cold War security system, and both have thus far come up lacking. Bilateralism, regional cooperation, and political caucusing by small and medium-size (hereafter medium) states in the alliance are responses to the hollowing-out of NATO. Another response is the push, driven by France and Germany, to give substance to a European security system centered on the ESDP. The paramount factor transforming regional security in Europe, especially in northern and central Europe, is the pull of bilateral relations with the United States in both positive and negative directions, fostering new alignment as well as resistance. In the coming years the region will remain a critical variable in the changing security architecture.

As the project of postcommunist institutional transformation gathered momentum in the 1990s, the residual structures of the North Atlantic Treaty Organization were the focal point, with progressively more emphasis on the norm-setting function of the alliance regarded as the vehicle for institutional reform.[3] The Clinton administration was willing to wager the viability of NATO's military function in order to focus on NATO's normative aspects as a means of assisting postcommunist transformation and stabilization in Central and Eastern Europe. NATO enlargement became the preferred vehicle for the new democracies' "return to Europe." But the price would prove steeper than expected, as NATO's political dimension began to overshadow its military utility. The fact that in northern Europe neither Sweden nor, more important, Finland expressed much interest in joining the alliance while they did join the EU in 1995, signaled the extent to which NATO was forfeiting its traditional military security function.

It has become a cliché of academic and policy discussions that in the course of what has been called dual enlargement of NATO and the EU the countries of North and Central Europe have become institutionally interconnected, but the institutional framing of the region tells only part of the story. Geography and history still matter, especially in a region that for more than a century found itself athwart the crosscurrents of political and military competition between Europe's great powers. It is in such a context that ever since the end of the Cold War the states of North and Central Europe have generated a new level of security cooperation driven by the confluence of national and regional interests. Those interests persist, informing the debates on the future of NATO and the ESDP. To put it differently, regional security policy considerations continue to matter during the present transitional period. They are even more apparent today, in the post–September 11 international security environment, than they were right after the end of the Cold War.

It is from the perspective of regional considerations that this book explores the changing levels of security cooperation among Germany, Poland, the Baltic states, and the Scandinavian countries, in terms of both traditional military-to-military and counterterrorism cooperation. The book also examines the role of Russia as a Baltic-rim power outside NATO and the EU, but one with continued important security interests and influence in the region. It explores how the intraregional dynamic has changed to accommodate the policies of the United States, especially in view of the way Washington has relied on countries from the region in its global strategy in the war on terror and the Second Iraq War, and how some countries opted for a EU strategy instead. In that context, the book outlines the possible range of security policy options available to the region, depending on the evolution of NATO and the EU and, most important, on U.S. security policy and changes in transatlantic relations.

AGGREGATING VS. STRUCTURING FUNCTIONS OF ALLIANCES

Historically, alliances have allowed states to pool their resources for common defense against common threats. This traditional aggregating function has often been augmented by the structuring function, whereby the very existence of an alliance orders the security relationships among its members, attenuating and containing the potential for regional conflict inside the alliance. While the aggregating function denotes defense burden-sharing—with smaller players drawing security payoffs that may far exceed their contribution and, in extreme cases, may lead to "free-riding"—the structuring function is a consequence of formal security arrangements within the alliance.

Small and midsize powers depend on alliances to structure their security environment far more than great powers or regional hegemons do. Within existing alliances smaller players factor in their regional security calculus, set the pattern of regional cooperation, and plan for action in conflict. Most important, membership in an alliance enables the smaller power to add to its defensive capabilities far beyond its indigenous capability. As alliances loosen and unravel, as has been the case with NATO since the end of the Cold War, small powers lose that essential security payoff. The problem does not always openly manifest, as has been the case in North and Central Europe since the disintegration of the Soviet Union because of the currently benign security environment.

In addition to strengthening the external security function, alliances enable states to shift their intraregional dynamic and make historic breakthrough shifts away from conflict to cooperation, especially in the context of a clearly identifiable external threat. The radically transformed post-1945 Franco-German relationship in the context of NATO is one example of how alliance membership can structure an intraregional security dynamic and lead to cooperation. During the Cold War the intensity of the external Soviet threat accelerated the internal structuring of NATO, transforming historically antagonistic relationships into cooperative ones. Even when divisions surfaced—for example during periods of tension and outright hostility between Turkey and Greece—the internal structuring function of NATO toned down the intensity of conflict and contained the potential for security competition between the two states. The external threat posed by the Warsaw Pact provided the impetus for NATO's internal structuring mission. To put it differently, the core business of NATO, i.e., containing the Soviet Union and defending against the Warsaw Pact, created the structuring function and its by-product the great success story of reintegrating Germany into Europe. The structuring payoff of American security guarantees to Europe during the Cold War would prove powerful enough to give NATO more than a decade-long run after the end of the Cold War.

Another important factor complicating discussion of the structuring role of alliances is the necessary distinction between wartime and peacetime conditions. Although Soviet-American Cold War competition in Europe never became an all-out armed conflict, it was a war nonetheless. Its end would inevitably lessen the sense of danger and the concomitant sense of urgency. In the 1990s the structuring function of the alliance would become the paramount mission. Under benign security conditions, different levels of threat perception produce different behavior by states, both inside and outside the alliance. From that perspective the end of the Cold War was a defining moment, setting a clear distinction between the Cold War and post–Cold War behavior of NATO members. Threats remained, but of a different kind. In place of Soviet military might, uncertainty about stability along the eastern periphery became paramount in the 1990s. Those concerns, albeit serious, never had the intensity associated with the Soviet threat during the Cold War.

In the past, alliances have given states opportunities to aggregate their power and structure relationships among them. Arguably the two biggest variables in how states will behave in an alliance are the overall level of perceived threat and whether the alliance or some of its members are at peace or war. NATO's predicament after September 11, 2001, was that policy choices by individual members, as well as actions by the alliance as a whole, created unprecedented confusion. On the one hand, on September 12, 2001, NATO invoked Article 5 of the Washington Treaty in defense of the United States after the terrorist attack on the World Trade Center, thereby treating the attack on the United States as directed against all members of the alliance. On the other hand, the United States chose to pursue its war in Afghanistan on its own, in effect declining to accept the collective-defense provisions of the Washington Treaty and turning to NATO for assistance in peacekeeping and support operations in Afghanistan only after the Taliban had been routed. Not surprisingly, the structuring function of NATO proved no match for responses generated by the Cold War–era Soviet threat. By the time NATO became involved in the International Security Assistance Force (ISAF) mission in Afghanistan the structuring function of the alliance had been largely disconnected from the capabilities aggregation function.

The separation of the alliance capabilities aggregation function from the structuring function has been the creeping pattern of NATO's evolution since the end of the Cold War. The result of the disassembling of the two functions has been twofold: (1) repeated efforts to find a different formula for aggregating capabilities in a way that would meaningfully match the threat perception through such formulas as the Prague Headline Goals or the NATO Response Force (NRF)—a high-readiness deployable force numbering some 21,000 when fully operational in October 2006, and (2) greater political caucusing—within the alliance reflecting fissures between the United States, France, and Germany; within the European Union itself, between the states that support and those that oppose American policy; and by way of new partnerships between the United States and some European NATO members, especially Poland and other postcommunist democracies.

For countries that are firmly embedded in EU structures and insulated from the immediate pressures at the Union's eastern boundary, NATO no longer presents itself as a premier security organization. By contrast, countries constituting the eastern Schengen frontier—that is, the area of the EU where border controls between states covered by the agreement have been abolished—consider the disaggregation of NATO's traditional defensive functions from the structuring functions to be a serious blow to their security; they take the view that the capabilities-aggregation function of the alliance far outweighs its structuring function. For the new members of NATO in Central Europe and the Baltic littoral, as well as for the Nordic countries—regardless of whether they are members—the recent memory of Soviet threat has generated a greater renewed sense of shared interests. Hence for example although Finland has no interest in joining NATO and has kept its distance from American policy in the

Middle East while Poland is arguably the most pro-NATO and pro-American state in the region, they both remain wary about Russia's intentions and see territorial defense as a continued concern. Notwithstanding their different power potentials and security policies, northern and central European states share to varying degrees geostrategic concerns by virtue of their proximity to the eastern boundary of the enlarged European-Transatlantic area. Denmark, the Baltic states, Poland, and to some extent even Germany (although its power by far surpasses that of other states in northern and central Europe) have had a strategic incentive to supplement their institutional cooperation inside NATO and the EU with bilateral cooperation either in the region or with the United States.

A different way of looking at regional security dynamics emerging since NATO's power aggregating and structuring functions have been separated is to consider the return of unilateralism and bilateralism beneath the umbrella of allied institutions. For instance, Poland's decision to seek a special relationship with the United States and the Baltic states' choice of pro-American policy during the 2003 Iraq crisis underscored the emphasis they placed on the capability aggregative function of NATO. Other states in the region, such as Finland and Sweden, have chosen to respond to their regional security concerns by supporting the European Union's plans for the ESDP while retaining viable territorial defense capabilities. While bilateral cooperation in North and Central Europe has proceeded apace, the extent of regional security cooperation is not yet clear, as the key states' disparity in power potential remains considerable. With the exception of Germany, the states that are the subject of this book are all small and medium powers that have neither the capability nor the political will to both "self-insure" and remain deeply invested in NATO and the ESDP. As a result, the security policies pursued by the northern and central Europeans do not lend themselves easily to neat theoretical categories but rather constitute a combination of initiatives aimed at retaining as much of both the power-aggregation function and the structuring function as possible, while developing their bilateral relations within the institutional context of NATO and the EU. That process is an important theme of this book.

States that are close to an area of potential instability and conflict have a higher level of threat perception than states that are more insulated by their geographical position. States cooperate not only because they are subject to a shared external threat but also because their perceptions of the nature of that threat coincide. As threat perceptions increase for one region within the alliance, states tend to balance against those threats by seeking alternative alignments or by generating a greater degree of security cooperation among them, including military cooperation.[4] For example, the role of the Scandinavians in creating and modernizing the armed forces of the Baltic states offers a good illustration of how shared perception about Russia generated cooperation; regional geostrategic concerns played themselves out below the institutional level of the alliance. To an extent, the continued existence of NATO after 1990 is best explained as a way of continuing the "structuring" function of the alliance and setting the context of Central Europe's reintegration not just with the rest of the Continent but also within the region. The important issue is that while NATO enlargement cannot be fully understood from the balance-of-power perspective, the structuring function of the alliance at the regional level is by definition much more tenuous than the capabilities-enhancing function. In fact, such an approach to alliance formation is likely to lead to the gradual hollowing-out of the alliance system, as the regional considerations in the boundary area often cannot be reconciled with security-threat perceptions deep inside Continental NATO. At best, all can agree that northern and central Europeans bring their additional local considerations to the table. At worst, the view of Russia's intentions and capabilities may prove contradictory, paralyzing the Europeans' ability to cooperate.

This book takes as its central theme emerging regionalism and bilateralism both in Europe and in transatlantic relations as the salient trend for the coming decade. The new dynamic has connected the security of North and Central Europe to an unprecedented degree. The book examines the core relationships in the region, identifying where the congruence of state interests facilitates greater military and political cooperation and where the disparity of power and differing threat assessments and relations with America have driven a wedge between key states in the region, specifically Germany and Poland. Next, it broadens the discussion of regional linkages around the Baltic littoral to include Scandinavia, where historical experience and residual security considerations bind NATO and non-NATO, EU and non-EU, and dual-NATO/EU members into a mosaic of shared regional cooperative arrangements. It covers the Baltic states, along with the added dimension of the Russian Federation and the Kaliningrad District as they affect regional security in North and Central Europe. The book concludes with a discussion of the critical element of the regional security dynamic, i.e., U.S. national security policy before and after September 11, 2001, with a special emphasis on the impact of the Second Iraq War on the region. Specifically, the chapters cover (1) an overview of the region; (2) German-Polish relations, treated as the region's core; (3) Scandinavian countries' security policies as the second tier of regional security cooperation, including NATO members as well as the EU non-NATO members (Finland and Sweden); (4) the Baltic states and Russia's Kaliningrad District; and (5) the key variable of U.S. policy in the region.

Finally, a word of explanation about the rationale for the limited scope of discussion of one important Baltic littoral state: the Russian Federation.

Russia is and will remain a Baltic power, with a set of vested interests and a historically defined perspective on its role in the region. Even so, , continued internal turmoil in Russia and the attendant unpredictability of its development constitute a threat to the region's stability and security. Rather than being part of the regional security structure, Russia is an external variable, and its policies, such as those regarding the Kaliningrad District, will continue to have an impact on the region's overall security configuration. In short, Russia is more a part of the problem than the solution.

NOTES

1. For background on ESDP and its evolution, see chapter five.
2. On the "coalitions of the willing" approach, see John C. Hulsman, "Cherry-Picking as the Future of the Transatlantic Alliance: The Reemergence of European Gaullism," in *The Transatlantic Relationship: Problems and Prospects,* ed. Sabina A. M. Auger, 59–66 (Washington, DC: Woodrow Wilson International Center for Scholars, 2003).
3. For example, Celeste A. Wallander and Robert O. Keohane, "An Institutional Approach to Alliance Theory" (working paper 95-2, The Center for International Affairs, Harvard University, Cambridge, 1995).
4. Patricia Weitsman argues that as threats grow from one state to another, "states have incentives to come together in an alliance in order to manage or constrain their alliance partners. This behavior, tethering, entails reciprocal or symmetrical threats— it does not represent the capitulation of one state to another, as does bandwagoning behavior. Yet if a threat from one state to another continues to grow, states will seek to secure themselves elsewhere, that is, they will balance against threats. If the level of threat grows to such an extent that a state's survival is on the line, the state will indeed capitulate to the greater threat and ally with the source of danger, that is, it will bandwagon." *Dangerous Alliances: Proponents of Peace, Weapons of War* (Stanford, CA: Stanford University Press, 2004), 4.

The Geostrategic Reconfiguration of North and Central Europe

LEGACIES AND DILEMMAS

*H*istorically, the idea of North and Central Europe has been a changing and often poorly defined concept, subject to shifting political alignments and changing power distributions in the region. During the Cold War Central Europe did not function as a geostrategic idea, with Germany divided between the West and the East and Poland being a satellite of Russia. Scandinavia and the Baltic littoral, albeit an important area of Cold War competition, lacked a larger shared security identity. The three Baltic states, Lithuania, Latvia, and Estonia, were occupied by the Soviet Union in World War II and separated from the North when the Soviet Union incorporated them directly. During that time Scandinavia was cleaved by often mutually exclusive institutional security arrangements: Sweden and Finland pursued military nonalignment—although based on different considerations in each case—while Norway and Denmark tied their national security to the North Atlantic Treaty Organization and America's security guarantees to Europe.

The legacy of World War II and the evolving dynamic of superpower competition directly defined the security policy choices of the Scandinavians. Norway chose membership in NATO but decided not to seek membership in the European Community (European Union), Denmark chose NATO and EC (EU) membership, but with opt-outs on European security and foreign-policy provisions. Sweden autonomously defined its military nonalignment as an extension of the idea of neutrality, while its cooperation with the West was broadly construed. Finland's "neutrality" was forced on it by its geostrategic position and the historical circumstance of post–World War II arrangements; throughout the Cold War Helsinki would not forget the history of the 1940 Winter War or the looming presence of Russia across its eastern border.

During the Cold War regional security in Europe was a by-product of superpower global political and military competition. In the process, North and Central Europe as a geostrategic region was subsumed by the larger East-West division embodied in NATO and the Warsaw Pact. Frequently, the mapping of European security made little historical sense. For example, set against the Cold War fault lines, historic European cities such as Prague and Warsaw found themselves situated in the political East, while Istanbul was in the political West. Scandinavia's security was defined within overlapping and at times confusing security commitments, framed by both nonalignment and NATO membership. At the heart of Central Europe, the two Germanys epitomized the conundrum of European and transatlantic security imperatives, with the internal German border becoming the defining fault line in the Cold War and transforming West Germany and East Germany into frontier states. Patterns of NATO and Soviet military deployment during the Cold War made the two German states the center of superpower competition. The Cold War, which had started with the division of Germany, ultimately ended with German unification.

Communist Poland, the largest non-Soviet Warsaw Pact member, was fully integrated into Soviet war-fighting plans with the Warsaw Pact's coalition-warfare strategy, notwithstanding its effort to gain a modicum of command autonomy through a "Polish front" idea in the run-up to the Pact reforms of 1969. Both Germany and Poland would have been the central battlefield if NATO and the Warsaw Pact had ever gone to war. During the Cold War, the burden of history in German-Polish relations constituted an added dimension to the security equation in the region. The legacy of Nazi wartime atrocities in Poland was never far from the mind of the Polish government or public. In Germany, the loss of territory transferred to Poland through the sanction of the 1945 Yalta agreement remained a central issue. Those bitter legacies of World War II froze German-Polish relations for more than two decades, and even after the 1969 rapprochement between Bonn and Warsaw mutual mistrust ran deep. Even today, after a decade and a half of policies aimed at German-Polish reconciliation, the past remains close to the surface of the new relationship, now and again emerging center stage. The Cold War–era superpower rivalry subsumed all other regional alignments, and even where efforts were made to initiate dialogue, the larger security architecture dominated regional considerations in North and Central Europe. Being a satellite of the Soviet Union, communist Poland could not pursue an independent national foreign policy. Although it emerged from the ashes of the Second World War as a democratic state, the Federal Republic of Germany had a national foreign policy circumscribed by the larger imperative of transatlantic alliance on the one hand and the intra-

European institution-building project on the other. The three pillars of Germany foreign policy—NATO, the EC (EU), and international multi-lateralism embodied in the United Nations—defined Germany's new place in the international system. During the Cold War, the security policies of both Poland and Germany were subsumed under the umbrella of Soviet-American competition. Central Europe as a historical and geostrategic region did not exist for forty-five years, cleaved as it was by the Iron Curtain and the ideological competition it symbolized.

Another consequence of the Cold War era was the disappearance of the Baltic littoral as the historic meeting ground of Europe's north, middle, and east. Because of their forced incorporation into the Soviet Union, the Baltic states did not factor into the regional security equation at all; after World War II Lithuania, Latvia, and Estonia were treated as a mere extension of the USSR. As the dominant political and military presence along the Baltic seaboard and in Central Europe, the Soviet Union itself constituted an ever-present threat to regional security in Scandinavia, for in a putative East-West conflict the Baltic region would have become part of the greater European theater of war. The East-West divide overshadowed the regional configuration within the Baltic littoral area, making the regional security equation relevant within the larger NATO–Warsaw Pact context, but beyond that having little connection to regional power distribution. Following the accelerated decomposition of Soviet control over its satellites that began in the late 1970s, the region began to "return to diversity."[1] Still, the revolutionary change in the regional security equation had to await the destruction of Communist Party power monopoly in Poland during the rise of the Solidarity movement.

After the 1990 unification of Germany the idea of Central Europe resurfaced and quickly took hold, with references to the nineteenth-century concept of *Mitteleuropa* to serve as a symbol of the final demise of the Yalta system. In the early 1990s the idea of Central Europe was qualified by adding the moniker "postcommunist" or by employing the term "East-Central Europe" in place of what analysts once had called the northern tier of the Warsaw Pact. Such distinctions rapidly faded, and after the 1997 NATO Madrid summit decision to invite Poland, Hungary, and the Czech Republic to join NATO, they were largely abandoned. The return of the idea of Central Europe to security debates on the emerging geostrategic configuration brought forth the inevitable question about the place of the Baltic littoral and its relations to the Nordic/Scandinavian region after Lithuania, Latvia, and Estonia declared their intention of joining both NATO and the EU. NATO's decision to enlarge restored the idea of Central Europe as corresponding to a geostrategic region and set the stage for connecting the Baltic and Scandinavian regions. Finally, NATO and EU enlargement conferred "frontier" status on Poland and the Baltic states, much in the manner of Finland vis-à-vis Russia and its "near abroad."[2]

The speed with which communism was overthrown in Eastern Europe in 1989 and the scope of the Soviet Union's collapse thereafter brought to the fore the core security dilemma for all small and medium powers in North and Central Europe and the Baltic littoral. Though in each case the set of issues was different and the overall capabilities varied—from affluent Germany and the Nordic states to the relatively poor Baltic states and Poland, the goal of fostering stability was shared across the region. The postcommunist democracies were in a particular predicament because for them the principal challenge was not only to secure their newly regained independence but also to address their dual insecurity dilemma, defined by the intersection of the region's geopolitics and capabilities. The new democracies' dilemma stemmed from the historical discontinuity of their state institutions on the one hand and lack of indigenous power to deal with external threats on the other. For Poland and the Baltic states in particular, the history of foreign occupation and the interruption of the institutional continuity of the state itself meant that reconstruction would not simply be democratic restoration but in effect would combine the political restoration of the states with the development of a workable regional security system. Postcommunist transition for those states would mean state building. Whereas in the area of political institution building those countries could reach back to their pre–World War II democratic experience and deeper democratic traditions, in the area of national security they would find less in their history to serve as the foundation of a workable system. Not surprisingly, NATO and EU membership became their key policy objectives from the start.

THE THREE SUBREGIONS

The post–Cold War North and Central Europe is a combination of overlapping geostrategic subregions, with Central Europe, Scandinavia, and the post-Soviet Baltic States pursuing policies that more often than not respond to similar regional pressures and aim at similar goals. The countries of North and Central Europe are diverse, with different historical legacies that have defined their national security optics. Since 1990 they have shared not only the political identity of democratic states but also several core security concerns. Such commonalities make it possible to talk about a larger North and Central Europe divided into three subregions: the core of Germany and Poland, the Nordic/Scandinavian tier, and the Baltic periphery. First and foremost, their proximity to the Russian Federation, especially to its Kaliningrad enclave on the Baltic Sea, ensures that their security policy will retain a greater sensitivity to the Eastern dimension than to that of Western European states. The memory of more than four decades of direct Soviet domination is never far away from the security policy considerations of the Poles or the Balts, nor is the memory of Moscow's pressure and the proximity of Russian military power far from the concerns of decision makers in Finland, Sweden, and Norway. Russia has also been and will remain a concern for Germany, even as the new German-Russian relationship offers Berlin future economic opportunities.

Another factor that ties the three subregions and the states in them together is the dual enlargement of NATO and the EU that occurred in 2004. That process conferred an unprecedented degree of institutional compatibility between the new and old members. Central Europe and the Baltic states became two subregions embedded in both NATO and the European Union. In the North, the Scandinavian countries offer a more complex picture, with Denmark a member of both NATO and the EU, Finland and Sweden in the EU but outside NATO, and Norway in NATO but outside the EU. Still, even though the institutional security framework in North Europe is not as uniform as in Central Europe and the postcommunist Baltic states, selective membership in NATO and the EU offers the Nordic/Scandinavian tier a degree of complementarity that has been an important factor in defining its security.

In addition to how they fit in the NATO and EU framework, the three subregions align and divide depending on how the individual countries relate to the United States. That has been an especially important structuring factor since the 2003 Second Iraq War, which generated sharply different responses among the governments in North and Central Europe. In the wake of the war Germany became one of the strongest opponents of American policy in the Middle East, while Germany's largest partner in Central Europe, Poland, became America's staunchest supporter. The degree of Poland's pro-Americanism is best illustrated by polling, conducted on the eve of the U.S. 2004 presidential election, which showed that Poland was the only country in Europe where President George W. Bush would have been handily reelected. While Poland has been the most vigorous supporter of the United States, other countries have shown a degree of support for American policy in the Middle East. The three Baltic states supported U.S. policy in Iraq. So did Denmark, which, like Poland, offered direct military assistance in the operation. In contrast to Copenhagen's support for Washington, the positions taken by Sweden and to a lesser extent Finland were critical of U.S. policy.

As the varied responses to the Iraq war demonstrated, reactions to American policy play an important role in generating cleavages within the three subregions. Last but not least, the three subregions can be differentiated in terms of individual states' security policies, especially their commitment to NATO and the EU's European Security and Defense Policy (ESDP). Preference for transatlanticism over the European security option is determined by the levels of public support as well as each country's historical legacy, generating different degrees of engagement with the NATO alliance and the European defense project. Though they all speak to the same set of residual and emerging security institutions, their national security policies differ in the extent of their commitment and their views of whether NATO or the ESDP has priority.

Some fifteen years after the collapse of communism, North and Central Europe has emerged as a distinct region with a set of residual security concerns, old problems, and new opportunities. The collapse of the Soviet Union also opened new security linkages between Central Europe and the Baltic littoral, including states that were NATO members and those that emphasized military nonalignment during the Cold War.[3] After two cycles of NATO enlargement, as well as the 2004 EU enlargement, the states of the subregion have become integrated and interdependent to an unprecedented degree. The subregion is now anchored within the framework of two key European and transatlantic institutions, though each country has a distinctly different position within them.

THE IMPACT OF NATO ENLARGEMENT

Two critical factors in creating the new North and Central Europe were the unification of Germany in 1990 and the disintegration of the Soviet Union in 1991. In historical perspective, however, the factor that had set the process in motion took place thirty-five years prior to the unification of Germany, when, on May 6, 1955, the then Bonn Republic joined the North Atlantic Treaty Organization. That date marked the beginning of restoring Germany to Europe's community of nations. It not so much set out the conditions of open-ended French military superiority over Germany—as some have argued because Chancellor Konrad Adenauer forswore any future ambition for Germany to acquire nuclear, biological, or chemical weapons—as set the context for lasting Franco-German reconciliation.[4]

German membership in NATO would prove to be an essential step in restructuring core security relations in Western Europe. Most important, by addressing the residual French concerns about German power, Germany's inclusion in NATO opened up the possibility of a fundamental change in Franco-German relations and Franco-German reconciliation after World War II. It also strengthened the pattern of Franco-German relations, whereby

Germany would yield to French leadership on European foreign-policy issues, notwithstanding Germany's overwhelming economic superiority. NATO's transatlantic dimension added the requisite element of America's open-ended security commitment to Europe as the overall framework for reconciliation. In that sense, Germany's joining NATO in 1955 proved revolutionary, generating sufficient reassurance in France and Western Europe overall to make reconciliation possible.

Buttressed by America's continued security guarantee to Germany within NATO, Franco-German reconciliation defined German foreign and security policy for the remainder of the Cold War, with its general thrust enduring well into the first post–Cold War decade, even after the collapse of the Soviet Union and the attendant reconfiguration of European security. It is testimony to the inherent robustness of the transatlantic security architecture embodied in NATO not only that the alliance would survive Soviet attempts in the 1970s to "decapitate" Europe by breaking the transatlantic linkage but also that it would continue after the Cold War. After 1991 it became an instrument for reintegrating the postcommunist area into Europe through a structured and conditional enlargement process.

NATO enlargement in 1999 and 2004 showed both the transformational effectiveness of its norm-setting capabilities and the watering-down of its military capabilities. As in the West during the Cold War, the 1999 and 2004 cycles of NATO enlargement partially denationalized control over the armed forces of new allies and contributed to democratic transformation in the region. In keeping with the ever-greater salience of the structuring function of the alliance since the Cold War, the unification of Germany became de facto the first round of post–Cold War NATO enlargement in all respects but the name. By the time enlargement into Poland, the Czech Republic, and Hungary came on the agenda, NATO had put in place a strong set of conditions for the new entrants. Even before that, in the September 1995 *Study on NATO Enlargement*,[5] support for democratization, the structural issues of civilian democratic control over the military, and eliminating conflict among states were considered the guiding priorities. Conditions for membership included democratic and market systems, no unresolved ethnic issues, civilian democratic control over the military, and the ability to contribute to common security. The relative level of candidates' success in meeting these requirements became a gauge of NATO's continued viability, as well as a clear indication of its new and increasing limitations. The latter became increasingly apparent in the area of military modernization, which lagged further and further behind the indisputably successful political dimension of enlargement.

The goals of maintaining Germany's connection to the United States within the transatlantic alliance and providing Germany with stability along its eastern border within a multinational organizational framework were important considerations for forging ahead with the 1999 round of NATO enlargement. In geostrategic terms, postunification Germany has acquired a vital stake in the security and stability of its immediate neighbors to the east. Poland in particular repositioned itself in Germany's security-policy optics. In 1990 the greatest security gain for Poland was that for the first time since World War II it was bordering a NATO country. Moreover, the unified Federal Republic of Germany has been a liberal democracy, anchored in intra-European and transatlantic structures. NATO's continued existence after the Cold War and the decision to proceed with enlargement to the east opened the door to a new German-Polish relationship. By the mid-1990s that relationship became an essential component of German security policy, while Germany promised to serve as a conduit to greater cooperation between Poland and the West through the so-called "Weimar Triangle": Paris, Berlin, and Warsaw.

NATO enlargement guaranteed that the unequal relationship of Germany and Poland would not be reduced to bilateralism but would play itself out in the larger context of a multilateral organization guided by transnational institutions and norms. The same dynamic would apply to the three Baltic states brought into NATO in 2004, where power disparity between them and Germany would be even greater. Poland's 1999 NATO membership and the Baltic states' 2004 inclusion in NATO made the frontiers of the former communist states also the frontier of Germany and the larger transatlantic community. Following the 2004 EU enlargement they would eventually become as well the Schengen frontiers of Europe.

An important factor in the enlargement process and the blending of regional boundaries with NATO/EU boundaries in the Baltic littoral has been the rejection of the military nonalignment option for the three Baltic states. For Lithuania, Latvia, and Estonia, neutrality was never a credible solution to their security needs and was rejected from the start. In light of the history of Russian domination and the USSR's destruction of Baltic statehood, NATO and EU membership offered the only viable approach to regional security. There was little in the Baltic states' experience with Russia during the early postcommunist transition to inspire confidence regarding Moscow's intentions, as the Balts grappled with such issues as the Russian ethnic diaspora in their countries and Russia's residual military power—especially Russian bases in the Kaliningrad District. It proved important that shifting Baltic-Russian relations also generated a determined response from the Scandinavian countries, especially Denmark, Sweden, and Finland, as well as support from Poland and Germany. The U.S. decision to assist the Baltics, in combination with regional European support, permitted the Baltic states to create military forces from scratch and bring them through several Membership Action Plan (MAP) cycles to successful inclusion in the 2004 NATO enlargement.

In the course of the 1999 and 2004 cycles of NATO enlargement, as well as the 2004 EU enlargement, the countries of North and Central Europe have achieved a degree of greater shared identity buttressed by the institutional overlap of European and transatlantic structures. After 2004, coupled with an unprecedented degree of economic growth, democratic consolidation, and overall political stability in Poland and the Baltic states, North and Central Europe became a region in its own right as never before. The sense of shared interests would carry on even after the considerable strain of quarrel over the Second Iraq War and support for America's Middle East policy. In North and Central Europe, a decade and a half of institutional NATO and EU enlargement bridged the historical discontinuity of state institutions in the former communist states, reconnected them to affluent Germany, and forged a renewed sense of shared interests along the Baltic seaboard.

NOTES

1. An expression coined in the aftermath of the collapse of Soviet power in eastern and central Europe by Joseph Rothschild, *Return to Diversity: A Political History of East Central Europe Since World War II*, 2nd ed. (New York & Oxford: Oxford University Press, 1993).

2. André Leibich, "East Central Europe: The Unbearable Tightness of Being" (working paper, International Security Studies at Yale University, New Haven, 1999), http://www.ciaonet.org/wps/lia01/.

3. I am grateful to Robert Dalsjö of the Swedish Defense Research Agency (FOI) for suggesting the term "militarily nonaligned" in place of the traditional concept of "neutrality" as applied to Sweden and Finland. The idea of military nonalignment better exemplifies the policies pursued by Sweden and Finland in the course of the Cold War, as well as providing a suitable starting point for analysis of their security policy options after the collapse of the Soviet empire.

4. Carl Cavanagh Hodge, *Atlanticism for a New Century: The Rise, Triumph, and Decline of NATO* (Upper Saddle River, NJ: Pearson-Prentice Hall, 2004), 6.

5. *Study on NATO Enlargement (September 1995)*, NATO Basic Texts, NATO Online Library, http://www.nato.int/docu/basictxt/enl-9501.htm.

• 2 •

The Linchpin: Germany and Poland

THE BURDEN OF HISTORY

$\mathscr{T}$he unification of Germany and the end of the Cold War brought into focus the torturous history of German-Polish relations and served as a seminal moment of change. In the Second World War, Nazi terror hit Poland with exceptional severity. The country lost six million of its citizens—one fourth of Poland's population. The Polish organized underground resistance against German occupation was numerically the largest and strongest in all Europe, with the Home Army controlled by the Polish government in exile in London numbering some three hundred thousand members. The tragedy of the 1944 Warsaw Uprising, suppressed by the Germans after two months of the Home Army's desperate resistance and in the face of Stalin's determined refusal to assist the Polish fighters, is an exceptionally bitter chapter in the history of German-Polish relations. The uprising, followed by Hitler's ordering the complete and systematic destruction of Warsaw and the murder of more than two hundred fifty thousand Polish civilians, remain to this day an important symbol of the past and an issue in bilateral German-Polish relations.[1]

Historically, German-Polish hostility dates back centuries. It intensified in the late eighteenth century, when neighboring great powers wiped the Polish-Lithuanian Commonwealth off the map of Europe by partitioning Polish territory. Prussia, one of the three partitioners, partook of the complete destruction of the Polish state. The intervening period, before the restoration of Poland's Second Republic in 1918, was marked by German-Polish tensions, as Polish national identity consolidated in opposition to German as well as Russian power. The tragedy of the Second World War and Nazi occupation—with personal wartime encounters between Poles and Germans feeding national stereotypes and animosities—strengthened Polish mistrust and suspicion of German intentions and made rapprochement difficult to achieve for decades. Only in 1970 would communist Poland begin to normalize its relations with the Federal Republic, and that in the context of détente in Europe.

On the German side, the principal grievance against Poland has focused on the Yalta-mandated loss of territory to Poland and the concomitant expulsion of ethnic Germans after the war. The Bonn Republic saw relations with Poland as part of the larger problems of overcoming the legacy of the Nazi past and Germany's gradual reintegration into Europe. During the Cold War, relations with Poland derived from the larger East-West relationship, a subset of issues that confronted the Federal Republic while the communist government in Poland maintained the fiction of the "progressive" German Democratic Republic as Poland's true German partner. Bonn's foreign and security policies after the Second World War came to rest on three pillars: (1) transatlanticism, centered on cooperation with the United States and membership in NATO; (2) reintegration into Europe within the institutional framework of the European Community (later the European Union), built around Franco-German reconciliation and buttressed by *Ostpolitik* after 1968; and (3) seeking international legitimacy by way of support for the United Nations, which Germany officially joined in 1973.

Throughout the Cold War and beyond, the NATO pillar remained the core of German security policy. Its critical importance was symbolized by the declaration of West German sovereignty on May 5, 1955, which was followed by the country's membership in the Atlantic alliance. In addition to NATO, the EC (afterward EU) pillar both facilitated and symbolized Germany's return to Europe. Germany's quest for international legitimacy had an added regional dimension during the Cold War because German UN membership was tied indirectly to Central European security issues. West Germany (FRG) and East Germany (GDR) could join the United Nations only after Bonn's *Ostverträge* (Eastern treaties) with Moscow and Warsaw in 1970, the Quadripartite Agreement on Berlin in 1971, and finally the "Basic Treaty" between Bonn and East Berlin, concluded in 1972.[2]

The Central European dimension of the Bonn Republic's security policy was never far from the larger international context because the burden of Germany's wartime past hung the heaviest in Central and Eastern Europe. The three pillars of German security policy remained in place throughout the Cold War, and their preservation created the conditions that would permit the unification of Germany in 1990. NATO and the EC (EU) proved to be the means through which West Germany could gradually find its way back into the international community and into the East after the Cold War. West Germany's record in the UN further buttressed the country's position and aided unification. In effect, the burden of World War II remained a defining factor in West German foreign and security policy, no less than the legacy of the war defined the security optics of Poland. That burden, combined with the potentially explosive residual territorial issue (one-third of Poland's territory had belonged to Germany prior to World War II), presented a challenge to both countries in the immediate postcommunist transition era. Policy choices by the German and Polish governments following the unification of Germany would therefore radically and, overall, positively transform Central European security.

One more factor complicated German-Polish relations during the Cold War. Both countries were Cold War frontier states, and neither could seek rapprochement without being keenly aware of its inherent limitations. Whatever policy initiatives they might undertake were set against a larger East-West context, with ever-present implications for superpower competition. As a liberal democracy, the Federal Republic of Germany had far greater policy latitude than did communist Poland, which remained firmly tethered to the Soviet Union and which had to defer to Moscow in all aspects of foreign policy. But even Bonn's foreign policy during the Cold War had to be defined by a degree of caution—what one observer called the "culture of reluctance"—in policy initiatives. Bonn deferred to the United States and France on matters of grand strategy, making national strategic interest synonymous with both transatlantic and European goals. When France and the United States conflicted, as in the 1960s, West Germany could only watch tension between them redefine the internal dynamic of NATO and found it hard to reconcile the countervailing pressures.

RAPPROCHEMENT IN THE 1990s

Polish-German reconciliation held the key to the future of Central Europe as a cohesive geostrategic region. Germany's support for Poland's inclusion in NATO and the European Union proved decisive in that regard. Several critical decisions marked political reconciliation between Berlin and Warsaw—the most critical on Germany's part being to remain within the established transatlantic security system as it integrated the five East German *Länder* into the Federal Republic. By doing that, Germany sent a clear message to Poland that it had no interest in reopening great-power competition in Central Europe. Even more important, Bonn accepted the Oder-Neisse line as the border between Germany and Poland, and the border issue would not be reopened. It proved a pivotal decision because the territorial shift of the Polish state to the west as a result of Yalta had been at the heart of German-Polish relations prior to 1990. Warsaw's most critical decision was to frame the emerging German-Polish relationship after the Cold War as a "second grand European reconciliation"—the term used by Krzysztof Skubiszewski, Poland's foreign minister at the time, when he compared the salutary potential of radically improved German-Polish relations to the transformation of German-French relations in the aftermath of World War II.[3] Skubiszewski recognized early on that Germany had adopted a cooperative policy toward its eastern neighbor. Soon Germany became a proponent of bringing Poland into NATO and the European Union. The key message, that Germany would seek a new partnership with Poland, came when Bonn opted not to go beyond the existing security institutions after unification. On the Polish side, the policy pursued by the first Solidarity governments and followed by the coalition SLD/PSL (Alliance of the Democratic Left and Polish Peasant Party) postcommunist government after the 1993 parliamentary election and its Solidarity successor never strayed from Skubiszewski's outline.

Warsaw's vision meshed with Bonn's policy, leading to the signing of two founding bilateral treaties between Poland and Germany in 1991 that confirmed the existing borders and outlined a new framework for good neighborly relations. The Border Treaty and the Good Neighbors Treaty became the key to the emerging security cooperation arrangement in Central Europe, and they opened the door to German-Polish cooperation. They transformed Germany from a historical threat to Polish sovereignty to Poland's doorway to the West and integration with Europe. The border treaty in particular was critical to Polish security because it did away with the Polish fears of German irredentism and sent a strong message that Bonn was committed to working for Poland's integration with Western Europe's economic institutions. Article 2 of that treaty contained a specific pledge for each party to respect the other's sovereignty and territorial integrity.[4] The June 17, 1991, "good-neighbor" treaty gave further impetus to German-Polish reconciliation because in return for Bonn's commitment to Polish integration in the European Community the Germans got Warsaw's official guarantee of German minority rights in Poland.[5]

A rapid increase in the volume of trade and German direct investment in Poland followed throughout the 1990s. Poland's exports to Germany rose from $5.143 billion in 1993 to $9.904 billion in 1999; its imports rose from $5.288 billion in 1993 to $11.583 billion in 1999.[6] In addition, Poland and Germany worked to open a dialogue about their past relations, especially regarding the German occupation of Poland in World War II. In 1997 those efforts led to an official exchange of archival documents by Poland's Main Commission for Research into Crimes Against the Polish Nation and the Federal Archives of Germany.[7]

Most important, however, the decade of cooperation began to change popular attitudes. In June 1999, the Center for Public Opinion Research (CBOS) in Warsaw published the results of a series of polls run between 1990 and 1999 on Polish attitudes toward the Germans and the Ukrainians. When in 1990 Poles were asked whether Polish-German reconciliation was possible, only 47 percent answered in the affirmative; by 1999 that figure had risen to 73 percent—a 26-percent increase over the decade.[8] In addition, in the five years between 1994 and 1999, the perception of the German minority in Poland was also improved: from 28-percent positive in 1994, to 32-percent positive in 1999. Meanwhile, hostility toward the German minority living in Poland dropped from 30 percent to 24 percent.[9] The positive view of Germany was clearly favored by the younger generation of Poles. It appeared that Skubiszewski's vision was becoming a reality.

The 1990s saw practical manifestations of the new spirit of cooperation between Germany and Poland, especially in security matters. The new diplomatic framework of Polish-German relations after 1990 led to close military cooperation, with Bonn becoming one of the most vocal advocates of Poland's membership in NATO. Germany also assisted Poland in the areas of equipment, maintenance, and training. Even though German-Polish relations subsequently frayed because of the 2003 Iraq war, military cooperation continued. The six-year Polish military modernization program, approved in January 2001, included the acquisition of German Leopard tanks, as well as technical cooperation and joint training. The most immediate sign of the new military relationship was the creation in September 1998 of the Northeastern Corps, a cooperative venture of Poland, Germany, and Denmark headquartered in the Baltic port city of Szczecin on the Polish-German border. It consists of three national divisions: In addition to a Danish division (eighteen thousand personnel), the Poles have contributed the Twelfth Mechanized Division from Szczecin (twelve thousand personnel) and the Germans their Fourteenth Mechanized Division from Neubrandenburg (eighteen thousand personnel).[10] The 150 officers serving with the corps' staff are permanently based in Szczecin, while the divisions remain in their home countries. Corps command rotates every three years, with the first command assignment having been entrusted to a Danish general, followed by a Pole and then by a German.

BREAKDOWN IN THE WAKE OF THE SECOND IRAQ WAR

The legacy of improved relations between Germany and Poland built in the 1990s was put to a severe test in 2003 by the Second Iraq War. The confrontation within the transatlantic relationship brought to the fore radically different views of U.S. policy in Iraq and strained the German-Polish relationship. One contributing factor in this process has been the generational change among the German political elite. With the arrival of the "sixty-eight" generation, Germany has begun to assume, albeit with considerable hesitation, a more independent role in world affairs. Chancellor Gerhard Schröder's emerging relationship with Russia's Vladimir Putin has raised concern in Warsaw about German-Russian cooperation "above the Poles' heads," thereby pushing Warsaw even closer to Washington.[11] The coming together of German and Russian political optics contributed to the unbalancing of Polish foreign policy. While in the 1990s Poland considered it imperative to be engaged equally with Europe and the United States, the growing rift between France and Germany on one hand and the United States on the other over Iraq became for Warsaw the moment of choice. Poland firmly sided with the United States; for the Poles European security and Polish-German relations have always been unequivocally predicated of American presence in Europe. From Warsaw's vantage point, this is even truer today, when NATO's military capabilities have been hollowed out by successive cycles of enlargement.[12] As is true to different degrees for Denmark and the Baltic states after Iraq, the transatlantic link has become Poland's first priority. While during the confrontation over Iraq Germany publicly opposed U.S. policy, Poland chose to assume the prominent role of America's new strategic partner in Central Europe. The price would be inevitable strain on the Polish-German bridge, but Poland did not hesitate to pay it.

Today, the Poles are engaged in a high-stakes game to leverage their new influence in Washington while minimizing the damage to their position with the EU. The way Poland adjusts to the inevitable pressures within the European Union will have considerable impact on the region. While Poland seems to have no intention of playing second fiddle to Germany, Germany is without question the stronger partner. At the same time, Germany's long-term interests dictate that its relations with Poland need to be strengthened. On the eve of the Iraq war, approximately 12 percent of German trade was with Eastern Central Europe—more than Germany's trade with the United States at the time. Poland had even more at stake here because Polish trade with the EU is above all trade with Germany.[13] If Poland needs Germany, however, Germany needs Poland. As German industry shifts production to Central Europe, EU enlargement has become important to the country's long-term economic growth. This is even more urgent in 2005, as Germany tries to come to grips with the high cost of domestic reform and continued high unemployment.

Finding a way to work together remains a high priority in both Berlin and Warsaw, though the relationship has cooled, perhaps long term. While Germany has expressed strong views on the Iraq issue, it has restrained its public criticism of Polish foreign policy, and Chancellor Gerhard Schröder encouraged the Poles to vote "yes" in the June 2003 EU referendum. Likewise, while Poland continued to "punch above its weight" in foreign relations, it was careful to nurture its German connection through vigorous diplomacy. The confluence of official celebrations of the sixtieth anniversary of the Warsaw Uprising in 2004 and the sixtieth anniversary of the liberation of Auschwitz in 2005 refocused the attention of Germans and Poles on the past. It showed that consolidating German-Polish relations in the present decade is likely to be more challenging than the laying of foundations for better relations was in the 1990s.

There is still time to repair the damage inflicted by the Iraq war and to deepen regional cooperation. Poland and Germany must come closer again, this time perhaps more as partners than in the 1990s when Poland was seeking Germany's support for its membership in NATO and the EU. In 2003 and 2004 Berlin seemed willing to meet Warsaw partway. In mid-November 2003 German foreign minister Joschka Fischer sent a strong message during his visit to Poland that Berlin wanted to restore regional balance. Speaking directly to Polish concerns, Fischer declared his continued support for "active American presence on the 'Old Continent,'" emphasizing that "the United States is for us all the most important partner outside Europe" and that the "transatlantic relationship is the key pillar of global peace and stability." Fischer pressed for continued German-Polish reconciliation, seeking to deflect Polish anger over a proposed memorial in Berlin to Germans expelled from Poland. Speaking on behalf of Chancellor Schröder and the "majority of the Germans," Fischer emphasized that there could be no questioning of "our [German] responsibility for our history."[14]

If the frayed Polish-German relationship is to be mended, the Poles will also need to compromise. Berlin's commitment to forge a more consolidated EU requires that Warsaw not only accept but endorse the policy as well. Iraq aside, Germany and Poland have different approaches to several important foreign-policy issues. Reflecting its regional focus on foreign policy, Germany is hardly enthusiastic about further NATO enlargement beyond Central Europe after 2004. Poland, on the other hand, championed NATO membership for the Baltics and has insisted that continued independence and sovereignty of Ukraine remains vital to its national security. The active and highly visible role played by Poland's president, Aleksander Kwaśniewski, in the 2004 "Orange Revolution" in Ukraine speaks clearly to Warsaw's priorities. With Ukraine in the balance, a middle ground needs to be found that would reconcile the German and Polish positions on future NATO enlargement.

Policy differences on Russia are likely to remain the most difficult area of German-Polish relations in the coming years. Russia remains a security concern in Warsaw, while Berlin sees greater potential for economic opportunity and political cooperation with Moscow. Here lies perhaps the most difficult challenge for Polish foreign policy: that the recent and vivid legacy of Russian domination must be balanced against the realization that better Polish-Russian relations are important to Poland's relations with Germany. Following the 2004 round of EU enlargement, Poland became the key EU frontier state in the East and a conduit for German trade with Russia. Improving Polish-Russian relations is the next step in building the larger regional security architecture in Central Europe. Considering Poland's torturous recent history, continued and credible American engagement in the region remains crucial to bridging the Polish and German positions on Russia. Conversely, Poland's long-term value to the United States as its new strategic partner would be significantly enhanced by a restored and strengthened German-Polish relationship. The task will not be easy, but stakes are too high for both Berlin and Warsaw not to address it.

In 2005 German-Polish relations reached their low point. According to polls published in Germany at the end of the year, only 6.6 percent of Germans would welcome a Pole as a neighbor. The polling results were even more poignant in that they reflected the views of the youngest segment of German citizenry.[15] The festering question of reparations has been reignited by claims and counterclaims from both Berlin and Warsaw, including the renewed search— launched independently by both the German and Polish governments—for the lost 1953 declaration in which, reportedly, the Polish communist government declared all Polish claims against Germany to have been satisfied.[16]

MILITARY CAPABILITIES OF GERMANY

The problems of German military reform can be summarized as follows: the lack of political will and the lack of money. The two are interconnected, and one would be hard-pressed to assign greater weight to one or the other. In 2004 the German economy was struggling with 4.3 million unemployed and sluggish growth. In late fall of 2004 Germany's finance minister Hans Eichel admitted that the government would have to raise its borrowing to €43.7 billion, a whopping 49-percent increase over the earlier projection of €29.3 billion. In effect, in late 2004 it became clear that Germany had virtually no chance of reaching the stated goal of no new borrowing by 2006. More important, it meant that in 2005 Germany would likely breach the stability pact of the euro for the fourth time in a row, exceeding the GDP limit of 3 percent imposed on the government deficit.[17]

As 2005 began, the economic conditions had not improved, and the budgetary picture remained bleak. It is in the context of a protracted budget crisis that Bundeswehr reform goals and the overall security policy of the Federal Republic should be considered.[18] An important fundamental constraint on the structure of German military reform is the continued commitment to universal conscription as an "indispensable requirement for the operational readiness, effectiveness and economic efficiency of the Bundeswehr." German security policy remains committed to the twin pillars of NATO and the EU, though it has evolved so as not to be "narrowed down to geographical boundaries" and is aimed at "safeguarding our security whenever it is in jeopardy." In practice, Germany's security policy doctrine anticipates out-of-area operations, provided they are "conducted within the context of collective security systems"—the condition that was vetted by the Federal Constitutional Court and German Bundestag and confirmed as compatible with the country's constitution.[19]

At its foundation, German security policy is framed by a commitment to multinationalism within existing security structures, making it impossible for the Bundeswehr to act independently of the UN, NATO, and the EU, save for specific evacuation or rescue missions. Germany's commitment to remain in NATO following unification—the decision that at the time greatly reassured its neighbors—has also been a framework for German military power. To put it differently, the core tenets of German security policy make it all but impossible for the country to act in a "coalition of the willing" formula if such a coalition is not sanctioned by one—and preferably all—of the three organizations.

Berlin's security policy recognized that although the end of the Cold War radically improved the regional security situation in Central Europe, that benign environment is not fully free of military or nonmilitary risks. Terrorism and religiously motivated fanaticism and the proliferation of weapons of mass destruction (WMD) remain central concerns. However, in the post–September 11 environment, German counterterrorist policies have been framed by the principles of multilateralism, emphasizing that the strategy must center on broad international antiterror coalitions as a means of preventing and combating the threat. Moreover, Berlin has been quite clear that "preventive measures" must not be misconstrued for "war." Rather, "preventive security" is interpreted to take into account political, economic, ecological, social, and cultural conditions. As the German security policy statement puts it, "it is not possible to guarantee security primarily or solely by military means."[20]

German security policy also emphasizes the need for the continued central role of NATO and the indispensable role of the United States to

European security. On the other hand, Germany supports the ESDP as a "necessary supplement" to NATO, but not as its substitute, and emphasizes the need to explore new opportunities for cooperation with Russia—especially in light of the 2002 decision to invite the Russian Federation to submit Russia as a full member of the G8.

German security and defense policy is based on three founding assumptions: (1) that continued transatlantic partnership and America's involvement in European security remain important, (2) that the ESDP will augment and strengthen the key NATO relationships, and (3) that an important legal and human-rights dimension remains central to German security policy and should be secured by the country's active participation in the UN and the Organization for Security and Cooperation in Europe (OSCE). Rhetoric aside, the Germans continue to regard NATO as the cornerstone of European security and the ultimate guarantor of a stable Europe, emphasizing both the collective defense aspect of the alliance and its ability to provide a forum for consultation. But that policy has become increasingly conflated with the desire to increase the country's "sense of ownership" of NATO. This is an important aspect in German security policy where its regional position is concerned, especially in its evolving relationship with Poland, because Berlin's continued commitment to NATO is taken in Warsaw as the desire to keep the United States engaged on the Continent—the central goal of Polish security policy.

The NATO dimension of German security and foreign policy has another aspect. The Bundeswehr is arguably more integrated in NATO than any other country's military force in the alliance. In part for that reason, the Germans believe that they have a special responsibility for shaping the direction of NATO's evolution. Hence Germany's overall support for and participation in the NATO Response Force (NRF) program, as well as the missile defense and defense against WMD initiatives are part of their defense policy. At the same time, Germany remains committed to pursuing military modernization in a manner compatible with ESDP objectives.

In effect, Germany's security and defense policy remains pulled in two directions—transatlanticism and continentalism, with an increasingly pronounced tilt toward the latter. The 2003 *Defense Policy Guidelines* emphasized more than ever the centrality to German security policy of building up the EU/ESDP component, with the ESDP described as a "decisive step towards Europe's deeper integration and enhanced capacity for action in security matters. The goal is the creation of a European Security and Defense Union as part of a fully developed Political Union."[21] That is central from the vantage point of Berlin's commitment to the European integration project. Germany has been an important force behind framing the ESDP and has strongly sup-

ported the EU's force goals, even as it has argued that Germany's military assets will continue to be available to both NATO and the EU. Inevitably, there
is a bit of a shadow game in this aspect of Germany's security policy, as Berlin
clearly seeks to place the ESDP on a more equal footing with NATO, especially when it comes to decision making. Moreover, the Germans speak of the
Bundeswehr's role as largely focusing on crisis management, conflict prevention, and support to allies in out-of-area operations.

Berlin's military and security policy has generated often conflicting in-
terpretations, with some scholars arguing that German military contributions
have been consistently underrepresented in policy debates in the United
States. As Klaus Becher pointed out, the Bundeswehr not only participated in
the 1999 NATO campaign in Kosovo but also started deployments outside
Europe in 2001. The Germans contributed 450 soldiers to Operation Enduring Freedom in Afghanistan, a WMD weapons unit in Kuwait, units to the
naval task force at the Horn of Africa and the Gulf of Oman, and deployed
450 sailors for NATO's Operation Active Endeavor in the western Mediterranean to protect sea lanes against terrorist attacks. By early 2004 there were
close to eight thousand German troops deployed for various out-of-area missions, with forty-five hundred deployed in the Balkans, Kosovo, and Bosnia-
Herzegovina. The most significant German contribution to out-of-area missions has been the deployment of two thousand troops in Afghanistan as part
of the German contingent to ISAF and at an air base in Uzbekistan as part
of the air support mission. According to Becher's estimate, about a hundred
thousand German soldiers have served in Bundeswehr operations abroad
since 1998, with international operations consuming approximately €1.5 billion (some 5 percent of German defense spending).[22] Indeed, the limited
numbers for individual military operations should be kept in perspective, as
they reflect political decisions of the government in the face of a reluctant
public. Because Germany's opposition to the war in Iraq has been the focal
point of the discussion in the United States about Germany's role in the war
against terrorism, it has often been forgotten that the Schröder government,
to its credit, had sent German troops abroad prior to Iraq despite the fact that
some two-thirds of the German public was opposed to any German combat
participation in such missions.

On the other hand, the decision to send only limited contingents of German troops for missions abroad also reflected continued reluctance to adopt a
more active policy, although Berlin showed unquestioned solidarity with the
United States in the aftermath of the September 11 terrorist attack. Germany's participation in the ISAF mission in Afghanistan in particular was of
operational significance but also a symbolic gesture toward America and a
sign of gratitude for America's support of Germany during the Cold War. It

was an important milestone for Berlin in light of the country's history, at once breaking the mold and setting clear limits. It is clear that Germany's participation in such operations would be limited by the fiscal and material constraints under which the Bundeswehr operates, as well as continued uncertainty about the country's proper place in the new international landscape. In addition to the political dimension, the limitation is due to the fact that the Bundeswehr badly needs to modernize by investing in new equipment and training in line with the new, international-missions orientation touted in the country's position papers on defense. Military modernization requires greater consolidation of Germany's defense sector with other European consortia to lower the cost of R&D and leverage the economies of scale. Although Germany recognizes the need to shift from the previous posture of conventional defense against an attack by another state on its territory to defense against terrorist threats, the challenge for 2005 will remain getting from here to there. The dual shortage of money and political will are likely to remain decisive.

GERMAN MILITARY REFORM

In 2001 Germany finally launched a major reorganization program for its armed forces, perhaps the most fundamental restructuring of the Bundeswehr since its creation in 1956. It was sparked by the independent commission report chaired by former President Richard von Weizsäcker published on May 23, 2000, which recommended among other things cutting the size of the Bundeswehr from more than 330,000 personnel to 240,000, with the number of conscripts in the armed forces reduced from 130,000 to less than 30,000.[23] More important, the *Weizsäcker Commission Report* recommended increasing the crisis rapid reaction operational forces from 60,000 out of 338,000 total in the year 2000 to 140,000 out of 240,000 in 2006.[24] The recommended reductions, especially changes in the conscription-based component of the Bundeswehr advocated by the Weizsäcker Commission, would have a profound impact on the country, considering that in 2000 the available pool of draftees was approximately 400,000. If fully implemented, the recommendations would mean "selective conscription" based on a lottery, higher pay for the conscripts, and the effective end of the Federal Republic's half-century tradition of maintaining the "citizen in uniform" idea that underlay the reborn German army.[25] It ran into political opposition from Chancellor Gerhard Schröder and Defense Minister Rudolf Scharping, both of whom favored retaining conscription.

The long-term implications of the proposed reform were the most difficult to accept. More important than bucking the established tradition of the "citizen-soldier," the *Weizsäcker Commission Report*'s recommendations would in effect transform the Bundeswehr from a territorial defense force within NATO into a force for global out-of-area intervention. That would require the overall rethinking of German security policy, starting with the question of whether the "culture of reluctance" still belonged in Germany's thinking of its place in Europe and the world. The gist of the report was a call for Germany to face up to the urgent need to transform the Bundeswehr from a conventional force for territorial defense into one that could respond to the most likely future missions, i.e., crisis prevention and crisis management. It raised the question of whether such a new Bundeswehr would have come uncomfortably close to American views about the use of military power. The interpretation was buttressed by the additional recommendations that Germany support the development of NATO's multinational reaction forces and concentrate resources to improve airlift, sealift, and air defense.

The reform plan that was finally offered by Defense Minister Rudolf Scharping modified the Weizsäcker Commission's recommendations by proposing to reduce the Bundeswehr to 285,000 by the year 2005, while retaining 90,000 civilian employees, versus the 80,000 recommended by the Weizsäcker. Scharping's plan accepted the recommendation to increase the number of professional personnel for crisis-management missions but retained conscription as the Bundeswehr's foundation, setting a target of 80,000 conscripts and reducing conscription from ten to nine months as of January 2002.[26] It announced major weapons-procurement programs for ten to twelve years, to include among others 180 Eurofighter aircraft, 134 NH Industries NH90 helicopters, 73 Airbus A-400M transport aircraft, and 80 Eurocopter Tiger attack helicopters.[27]

The Scharping reorganization, including further changes introduced by Defense Minister Peter Struck, meant chiefly reductions, the brunt of which would be borne by an army slated to shed more than 100 battalions and several brigade and divisional headquarters, reducing its numbers from 230,000 to 190,000 over the next few years. The goal was to reduce the total numbers while doubling the number of personnel available for crisis-management missions. The new German army would be based on five mechanized divisions instead of seven, serving as both the basis for mobilization and a source of a reinforced mechanized division of some 35,000 available for NATO operations, yet without the necessity to mobilize. Most important, reductions that preserved conscription meant that Germany was not ready to move to the proactive vision offered by the Weizsäcker Commission.

The original Scharping plan clashed with the reality of the country's shrinking defense spending. Defense Minister Peter Struck revised Germany's defense reform goals downward to accommodate the fact that there would be no increase in defense spending before 2006. Under the Struck plan, announced first at a January 13, 2004, press conference, the Bundeswehr's peacetime strength would drop from 285,000 to 250,000 by the year 2010, and the number of civilian employees would shrink to 75,000 (below the targets recommended by the Weizsäcker Commission). Under the Struck plan, the Bundeswehr would be divided into reaction forces of 35,000, stabilization forces of 70,000, and support forces of 137,500 personnel. Significantly, the reaction forces would be the core of Germany's operational army. Approximately 15,000 of the 35,000 reaction forces would be available to rotate through the NATO Response Force, 18,000 would be available for other tasks within NATO and EU, and 1,000 would be earmarked specifically to conduct evacuations of German nationals in crisis. The stabilization forces would be prepared for multinational operations, such as ISAF in Afghanistan or the Balkan operations, with the goal of having 14,000 troops available for up to five simultaneous operations. Struck recommitted the government to relying on nine-month conscription but stipulated that the new structures would rely on a greater number of volunteers.[28] In effect, Struck's plan set the issue of the draft-based Bundeswehr aside, making it a prime political issue for after the 2006 election.

The key question for the German military reformers will be whether to retain conscription or move in the direction of a professional military. The German defense budget continues to absorb the high personnel costs, but the argument for professionalization instead of conscription needs to be made in terms of expertise instead of simply relative cost. In the aftermath of the 2003 Iraq campaign Foreign Minister Joschka Fischer publicly raised the idea of moving in the direction of professionalization, but it remains doubtful whether there would be sufficient public or elite support for such a change. Financial constraints constitute a persistent problem for German military modernization. For instance, though the Bundeswehr urgently needs to upgrade its airlift capabilities, the contract for the delivery of sixty Airbus Industries A400M transport aircraft between 2010 and 2016 is for thirteen fewer aircraft than originally planned,[29] and the first squadron of twelve new German A400Ms will not be operational until 2012.[30] The dilemma of the Bundeswehr is that it needs to undertake a major modernization program at a time when the resources available for it are insufficient. For Germany's defense industry to weather the tough times, consolidation partnerships with other European corporations would be required, along the lines of the Franco-German-Spanish EADS in the aerospace sector, and it would have to increase exports of its most successful products, such as the Leopard 2 MBT.[31]

In the end, money remains key to both transforming the German armed forces into a professional military and providing it with the requisite airlift and other necessary equipment for out-of-area operations. Without a substantial increase in German defense spending, even the existing acquisition programs, such as the contract for 180 Eurofighters, will have to be reduced further. Most important, the fate of German military modernization is key to the future of NATO as a viable military organization. For NATO to remain militarily viable, the German modernization effort must be conducted in close cooperation with the United States, to yield systems that require continued transatlantic cooperation—such as, for instance, the German-Italian-United States Medium Extended Air Defense System. Without such integration, interoperability will suffer, and NATO will lose even more rapidly its ability to muster combined military resources for joint power projection missions, thereby accelerating the current centrifugal pressures driving Europe and America apart. That makes the political estrangement with the United States in the run-up to the Iraq war all the more regrettable.

POLISH DEFENSE REFORM AND
MILITARY MODERNIZATION

In 2001 the Polish Parliament (*Sejm*) adopted the 2001–2006 Defense Plan for reorganizing and modernizing the Polish armed forces. The program was introduced in the wake of the failure of an earlier 15-year plan "The Army 2012," adopted by the Sejm in 1997 but subject to intense and bitter critical debate.[32] That program envisioned reducing the Polish armed forces from 220,000 to 180,000 by 2004. As early as 1998, however, the defense minister had declared the plan to be significantly beyond the resources available from budgetary allocations.

Like the German policy, the general thrust of the 2001–2006 Polish reform program is to prepare the armed forces for three core tasks: (1) defense in case of war; (2) crisis response, including Poland's participation in international missions; and (3) peacetime stability and preventive operations. The program commits the country to maintaining defense spending at 1.95 percent of GDP, with equipment purchases rising from 8.3 percent in 2001 to 22 percent of the total by 2006.[33] As in the German case, the bulk of personnel reductions has fallen on the army. The Polish land forces were reduced to 89,000 by 2003, and approximately 40 percent of infrastructure and obsolete equipment was eliminated. The equipment left to the Polish land forces would be sufficient for 48 battalions, including 27 mechanized units and 21 tank battalions, thus yielding 14 brigades, seven of which would be mechanized and six armored, plus one coastal infantry brigade. In short,

Poland will be able to field four divisions, rather than six as had originally been planned.[34]

As in Germany, conscription remains a central problem in Polish defense reform. One of the solutions proposed by Defense Minister Bronisław Komorowski during the discussions preceding the adoption of the reform program on January 31, 2001, was to reduce conscript service to 9–10 months after 2004.[35] The draftees would be assigned to areas requiring less training, such as infantry, guard duties, or drivers. The key roles in the new military would then be filled by so-called "contract soldiers," especially professional noncommissioned officers. The Poles have clearly modeled their contract system on the experience of the U.S. armed forces, with core expert functions performed by sergeants and staff sergeants.

The 2001–2006 Polish military reform stipulates phased-in deep personnel cuts: by 2001 the army was reduced to 180,000, by 2002 to 165,000, and by the end of 2003 to the target ceiling of 150,000, of which 75,000 were professionals.[36] The 150,000 ceiling was in place in 2004, as planned, though the scope of professionalization remained subject to debate. The current program stipulates the division of the Polish Armed Forces into two components: operational forces (*Wojska Operacyjne*) and territorial defense forces (*Wojska Obrony Terytorialnej*). The operational-forces component reflects the effort of military modernization of the past decade, including key decisions on hardware purchases, a focus on troop mobility, and a shift toward professionalization; a new law on professional military service was introduced on September 11, 2003.[37] The territorial defense component is and will remain largely conscript-based, which suggests that the Poles, though they plan to retain it, will assign conscription a secondary role in the defense system.

Compared to Hungary and the Czech Republic (the other 1999 NATO entrants), Poland has achieved the most in terms of military modernization, but it is still very much a work in progress. The 2001–2006 Polish defense reform program has committed 1.95 percent of GDP annually for defense. In early 2005 the goal appeared realistic, as the Polish economy grew in 2004 by 5 percent. The government projected the growth rate to be about 5.5 percent in 2005, notwithstanding the strengthening of the zloty against the U.S. dollar.[38] The force reductions have run their course, stabilizing at 150,000, with the retirement of all remaining T-55 tanks and MiG-21 aircraft and the acquisition of a new wheeled armored personnel carrier and a new multipurpose aircraft.[39] In December 2002 Poland selected a bid from Lockheed Martin to supply its air force with 48 F-16 aircraft. That "contract of the century" is valued at more than $3.5 billion.[40] The Polish land forces implemented personnel reductions and partial reequipment, including the transfer of Leopard 2 A4 tanks from Germany. The government also signed a contract for the delivery and subsequent manufacturing of the Finnish Patria, a wheeled APC. Still, the modernization of the Polish armed forces has a long way to go. Except for small pockets of excellence, such as the GROM Special Forces unit that performed very well in Iraq, the Polish armed forces are in need of substantial material investment. As became clear in the run-up to the deployment of the Polish-led division in Iraq, Poland has neither the airlift capability nor the equipment to sustain long-term operations outside its territory. However, notwithstanding their limited resources, the Poles remain serious about modernizing their military and cooperating with the U.S. armed forces.

In 2004, 30,000 of the 150,000 Polish military personnel maintained high readiness levels. One critical new element in the modernization process was the added value of the experience of the Polish forces serving in Iraq. In September 2003, Poland assumed command of a multinational division in Iraq, contributing initially approximately 2,400 personnel. By the end of 2004, Poland had implemented three rotations in Iraq, in the process accumulating invaluable experience for international missions, especially interoperability with the U.S. forces, and logistical support. The fourth rotation of the Polish contingent, led by Gen. Waldemar Skrzypczak, was formally dispatched for Iraq on January 4, 2005.[41] With each rotation, Poland's pool of experienced professional military personnel has increased, making it possible for Poland to plan to have a reservoir of some 30,000 professional officers and men for out-of-area missions.[42] The operation in Iraq, while placing a considerable strain on the Polish armed forces and requiring considerable sacrifice of the country's limited defense funds, also helped introduce updated equipment and procedures into the Polish military. Moreover, since the Polish deployment in Iraq was supported by NATO, the Poles gained invaluable experience working under difficult conditions according to NATO procedures.

The importance of the Iraq operations for Polish military modernization cannot be overstated, even though Poland is still unable to sustain the current force without American assistance. Iraq has become an important training ground for the modern Polish army, which is even more important when one considers that in 2004 the Land Forces constituted 60 percent of the entire Polish military.[43] But the political price that Poland has paid for the experience, especially in its relations with Germany, has been steep.

GERMAN-POLISH RELATIONS AFTER IRAQ: THE CONSEQUENCES OF CHOICE

The rift within the Atlantic alliance in the wake of the U.S. decision to go to war in Iraq proved especially damaging to German-Polish relations. Chancellor

Gerhard Schröder's decision not to participate in the military campaign under any circumstances contrasted sharply with Poland's decision to side with the United States. The ensuing "op-ed diplomacy,"[44] whereby a number of European countries, including Poland, published an open letter supporting the American position, further chilled German-Polish relations. Two critical developments took place during the intra-allied confrontation over Iraq that would shape the Central European security equation: It marked Germany's coming into its own on foreign policy,[45] as Chancellor Schröder strongly asserted in March 2003 in the Bundestag,[46] followed by an address to the public after the U.S. operation had begun that "Germany would in no way participate in this war."[47] That position not only directly contradicted the policy of the United States but also declared nonparticipation under any conditions. Germany agreed to contribute only to humanitarian relief if that were duly authorized by the UN. For Poland the very fact of making the choice was a dramatic departure from the country's position in the 1990s, as Poland had built its postcommunist foreign policy on the core assumption that it needed strong relations with both Germany and the United States.

The strain in German-Polish relations was further compounded by arguments over the new EU constitution, with Poland asserting that it would not compromise on the Nice voting agreement and Germany pushing for concessions. In the confrontation over Iraq, Germany publicly opposed the U.S. policy while Poland assumed the prominent role of America's new strategic partner in Central Europe, accepting the inevitable strain the policy would place on the Polish-German bridge. At the same time, however, Germany's long-term interests dictate that its relations with Poland be strengthened. Thus the German-Polish confrontation over Iraq and its aftermath, though often intense, was ultimately modified and contained by the existing institutional structures of NATO and, after May 1, 2004, Poland's membership in the European Union. However, perhaps because of the experience of cooperation during the heady decade following German unification, there is a growing hardening of attitude, at times accompanied by a sense of betrayal.

Polish-German relations have been at the center of the new security dynamic in the region. The end of the Cold War marked the emergence of Germany as one of the victors: Unification has transformed the country into the most powerful state on the Continent, as well as the dominant player in Central Europe. The implosion of the Soviet empire and the continued weakness of Russia have amplified the relative strength of Germany. At the same time, Germany's policy of preserving and expanding its existing security and economic institutions has offered Poland a historic opportunity to redefine relations between the two countries.

German economic stakes in the expansion and stabilization of the EU cannot be overstated; the EU accounts for more than half of all German trade. Although Germany is by far the stronger state and the most important trading partner for Poland, accounting for about a third of Poland's foreign trade, Berlin has a vital interest in maintaining good relations with Warsaw. Poland is Germany's second largest neighbor, and it has the largest market among the 2004 EU accession countries. With the Czech Republic, Poland is Germany's principal trading partner in Central and Eastern Europe. According to official German government statistics, in 2003 the total turnover of trade between Germany and Poland was €32.2 billion, with Germany exporting €16 billion to Poland and importing approximately the same amount for the year. Germany officially ranks fourth in terms of direct foreign investment in Poland, behind France, the Netherlands, and the United States.[48] However, in a full accounting of small-scale German investment in several thousand Polish small businesses, Germany would likely be considered a leading investor in Poland. The dual NATO and EU enlargements have not only served the purpose of stabilizing Germany's eastern periphery but have also set the conditions of German economic expansion into the region. Poland will be central to that process.

Like Germany, Poland has a vital national interest in bringing about the "second grand European reconciliation," to use Krzysztof Skubiszewski's term. Both states face a formidable historical burden, but as the victim of German aggression in World War II, Poland has a more difficult task when it comes to building a new foundation of mutual trust. Alongside Germany, Poland is a linchpin state to regional security in Central Europe. As an emerging middle power strategically located between Germany, the successor states of the Soviet Union, and the Baltic-Nordic region, Poland can play an important bridging role in regional security. In order to leverage the benign post–Cold War European security environment, Poland had to transform its historically adversarial relations with Germany. Any such bridging by Poland had to presuppose both continued German commitment to transatlanticism, and, equally important, American commitment to European security. Until the fracturing of the transatlantic community in the run-up to Iraq in the winter of 2003, Poland's German policy never strayed from the outline offered early on by Foreign Minister Skubiszewski to seek Polish-German reconciliation in the context of the existing Euro-Atlantic institutions, as Poland needs both Europe and America to overcome the past.[49] Taken in the context of continued U.S. presence in Europe and Germany's commitment to work for Poland's integration into NATO and the European Union, the 1990s laid the foundation for a lasting change in bilateral Polish-German relations.[50]

Despite the tension since 2003, the German-Polish relationship seems to have accumulated a sufficient amount of political capital since 1990 to be able to overcome the current low point. There is clear recognition in both Berlin and Warsaw that the two countries share common security interests in the region, as manifest by Germany's support during Poland's application for membership in NATO and the European Union. Likewise, Germany's unconditional admission of responsibility for the suffering of the Polish people during the Second World War, regardless of the continuing debates over compensation, remains central to continued reconciliation. In the end, Germany and Poland are today both members of the core security and economic organizations on the Continent.

NOTES

1. For a comprehensive history of the Warsaw Uprising, see Norman Davies, *Rising '44: The Battle for Warsaw* (London: Viking Penguin, 2004).

2. I am grateful to Dr. Detlef Puhl of the George C. Marshall Center in Garmisch, Germany, for pointing out the linkage between Bonn's regional policy initiatives and West Germany's UN membership.

3. "Wielkie zmiany" [Great changes], *Sztandar Młodych*, April 19–21, 1991.

4. "Polska i RFN podpisały traktat o potwierdzeniu istniejącej miedzy nimi granicy" [Poland and the FRG Signed a Treaty Confirming Their Current Border], *Polska Zbrojna*, November 15, 1990.

5. Francine S. Kiefer, "Germans Move to Reassure Eastern Europe," *The Christian Science Monitor*, June 19, 1991.

6. *IMF Direction of Trade Statistics Yearbook 2000* (Washington, DC: International Monetary Fund, 2000).

7. *Rzeczpospolita*, "Polsko-niemiecka wymiana dokumentów," June 19, 1997. The Germans handed over to the Poles the original files of the General Government (German government of Polish territories in World War II), and the Poles handed over a portion of the files of the General Directorate of Security of the Third Reich (RSHA).

8. *Polacy o możliwości pojednania z Niemcami i Ukrainą* [The Poles on the prospects of reconciliation with Germany and Ukraine] (Warsaw: CBOS, 1999), Komunikat #2154, June 28, 1999.

9. *Stosunek do mniejszości narodowych* [Attitude to national minorities] (Warsaw: CBOS, 1999), Komunikat # 2192, September 9, 1999.

10. Polish Press Agency PAP, "Poland, Denmark and Germany Sign Military Accord," news release, September 5, 1998.

11. Ilya Prizel, "Putin's Russia, the Berlin Republic, and East Central Europe: A New Symbiosis?" *Orbis* 46 (Fall 2002): 685–99.

12. Author's interviews with Polish government officials, Warsaw, May 2004.

13. Author's interviews with Polish government officials.

14. *Rzeczpospolita*, "Wielka Europa Joschki Fischera" [Great Europe of Joschka Fischer], November 14, 2003.

15. Telewizja Polska, *Linia specjalna*, TVP broadcast, December 18, 2004.

16. *Frankfurter Allgemeine Zeitung,* November 4, 2004.

17. *Frankfurter Allgemeine Zeitung,* October 1, 2004.

18. The following section is based on *Defense Policy Guidelines* (Berlin: Bundesministerium der Verteidigung, May 21, 2003), promulgated by Defense Minister Peter Struck. Hereafter referred to as *2003 Defense Policy Guidelines.*

19. *2003 Defense Policy Guidelines,* 3.

20. *2003 Defense Policy Guidelines,* 8.

21. *2003 Defense Policy Guidelines,* 11.

22. Klaus Becher, "German Forces in International Military Operations," *Orbis* 46, no. 3 (Summer 2004): 398.

23. Richard V. Weizsäcker, Peter-Heinrich Carstens, Theo Sommer, Christian Bernzen, Christoph Bertram, Ignatz Bubis, Eckhard Cordes, et al., *Gemeinsame Sicherheit und Zukunft der Bundeswehr. Bericht der Kommission an die Bundesregierung* [Common Security and the Future of the Bundeswehr. The Commission's Report to the Federal Government] (Berlin: Kommission "Gemeinsame Sicherheit und Zukunft der Bundeswehr," 2000). Hereafter referred to as the Weizsäcker Commission Report.

24. Weizsäcker Commission Report, 55.

25. Rüdiger Moniac, "Leaked German Report on Armed Forces Sparks Policy Row," *Jane's Defence Weekly,* May 17, 2000.

26. Joris Janssen Lok, "Germany Looks to the Future," *Jane's Defence Weekly,* August 8, 2001.

27. Rüdiger Moniac, "German Defence Row," *Jane's Defence Weekly,* September 20, 2000.

28. Jürgen Erbe and Andrew Koch, "Germany Will Streamline Forces to Boost Readiness," *Jane's Defence Weekly,* January 23, 2004.

29. *Jane's Defence Weekly,* "Germany Cuts Budget: But Clears A400M for Takeoff," December 6, 2002.

30. Jürgen Erbe, "Germany Approves A400M Airlifter Purchase," *Jane's Defence Weekly,* May 28, 2003.

31. *Jane's Defence Weekly,* "Balancing Act: Modernization Under Threat," April 11, 2001.

32. Marcin Mróz, "*Program przebudowy i modernizacji technicznej sił zbrojnych RP w latach 2001–2006*" w świetle informacji Rady Ministrów o jego realizacji w 2001 roku, Warszawa: Kancelarja Sejmu, Biuro Studiow i Ekspertyz, Raport Nr. 197, 2001.

33. Grzegorz Holdanowicz, "An Uphill Task," *Jane's Defence Weekly,* September 26, 2001.

34. Janusz B. Grochowski, "Armia 2006," *Polska Zbrojna,* n.d., at www.polska zbrojna.pl/artykul.html?id_artykul=263.

35. Artur Golawski, "Armia z przyszłoscią" [An Army with a Future], *Polska Zbrojna,* n.d., at www.polska-zbrojna.pl/artykul.html?id_artykul=234.

36. Mróz, 6.

37. Republic of Poland, Ustawa z 11 września 2003 r. o służbie wojskowej żołnierzy zawodowych [The Law of 11 September 2003 on the service of professional soldiers], *Dziennik Ustaw,* nr. 179, poz. 1750.

38. *Rzeczpospolita,* "To był dobry rok" [This was a good year], December 31, 2004.

39. *Rzeczpospolita,* "Gonimy sojuszników" [Catching up with the Allies], January 31, 2001.

40. *Rzeczpospolita,* "Amerykańskie skrzydła dla Polski" [American wings for Poland], December 28, 2002.

41. Ministerstwo Obrony Narodowej Rzeczpospolitej Polskiej. Warsaw, Poland, at www.mon.gov.pl.

42. Briefing, Polish Land Forces Command, Warszawa, Cytadela, May, 2004.

43. *Podstawowe informacje o budżecie MON na 2004 rok* [Key information on the budget of the Ministry of Defense for 2004] (Warsaw: Ministerstwo Obrony Narodowej, Departament Budzetowy, 2004).

44. The term used by Antonio Missiroli, "Central Europe Between the EU and NATO," *Survival* 46, no. 4 (Winter 2004–05): 128.

45. *Tagesspiegel,* "Es gibt eine friendliche Alternative" [There is a peaceful alternative], February 14, 2003.

46. Gerhard Schröder, "Mut zum Frieden und Mut zur Veränderung" [The Courage for Peace and the Courage to Change], *Regierungserklärung von Bundeskanzler Gerhard Schröder am 14. März 2003 vor dem Deutschen Bundestag* [German Chancellor Gerhard Schröder's policy statement addressing the Lower House of the German Parliament on 14 March 2003] (Berlin: Willy-Brandt-Haus Materialien, March 17, 2003).

47. Patrick Keller, "Germany Update," *Konrad Andenauer Stiftung* 7 (March 2003): 1.

48. Auswärtiges Amt [Foreign Office (German)], "Relations Between Australia and Germany," April 2004, at www.auswaertiges-amt.de/www/en/laenderinfos/laener/laender_ausgabe_html?type_id=14&land_id=13.

49. "Wielkie zmiany."

50. "Polska i RFN."

The Northern Boundary: Scandinavia

THE LEGACY OF SWEDISH NEUTRALITY

$\mathcal{T}$he end of the Cold War and the breakdown of the Soviet Union were a revolution in the security of the Nordic-Baltic region. First, they restored the sovereignty of Lithuania, Latvia, and Estonia. The three Baltic States had been forcibly incorporated into the Soviet Union as a result of the Ribbentrop/ Molotov Secret Protocol of 1939 and reabsorbed after the Soviet victory over Nazi Germany. The end of the Cold War also dramatically reduced the vulnerability of the Scandinavian states. The extension of Soviet power deeply into central Europe, including the partition of Germany in 1945 and the creation of the Warsaw Pact a decade later, had exposed the Scandinavians to forty-five years of pressure along the Baltic littoral. The Soviet threat placed the idea of neutrality—whether by choice, as in the case of Sweden, or by necessity, as in the case of Finland—in the forefront of thinking about regional security.

For Sweden, the largest Nordic power with a long history of influence in the Baltic in its own right, Soviet ascendancy along the Baltic coast after World War II, combined with the overall devastation of most of Europe, posed a direct threat to its security. It was made more compelling by the postwar exhaustion of Great Britain and the as yet uncertain American commitment to transatlantic security. The push for Sweden's neutrality during the Cold War was buttressed by its history of neutrality in both the First and the Second World Wars. After World War II, Sweden again sought refuge in its post-1812 "small power realism" that had since been the foundation of Stockholm's claim to neutrality.

Yet Sweden's neutrality was never absolute. Historically, Sweden's self-imposed neutrality was always modified by self-imposed limits. When vital national interests were at stake, for example during the Finnish-Soviet Winter War of 1940, Sweden had shifted its position from "neutrality" to "non-belligerence"—an important distinction reflecting the country's concern about its eastern flank in the event of Finland's complete subjugation by the Soviets. Hence, during the Winter War Sweden supplied Finland with weapons and munitions, extended credit, and provided volunteers, although Stockholm stopped short of outright military assistance to the Finns.

As the Winter War demonstrated, Swedish neutrality was more precisely a matter of "military nonalignment" that remained highly sensitive to the region's geostrategic context. Furthermore, Stockholm purchased this military nonalignment at the price of substantial military outlays so as to maintain a modicum of deterrence. It is debatable whether Sweden's military was by itself the reason the country was spared occupation during World War II, as Stockholm frequently resorted to political compromise to buttress independence. The policy of military nonalignment combined with robust defense capability continued after the war. Sweden even began to pursue a nuclear weapons program in 1949, two years after the civilian atomic agency (*AB Atomenergi*) was established, with the goal of enhancing the country's nuclear capabilities. The program lasted until 1968 when the Parliament made the decision to abandon it, though some R&D continued.[1] In addition to maintaining autonomous defense capabilities, Stockholm explored a Nordic regional security arrangement by proposing (unsuccessfully) a Defense Union with Norway and Denmark, with Finland excluded on account of its tenuous position vis-à-vis the Soviet Union and the constraints inherent in the 1948 Treaty of Friendship, Cooperation, and Mutual Assistance imposed on Helsinki by Moscow.

One important aspect of Swedish military nonalignment was an implicit premise of political alignment with the West. If attacked, Sweden would side with the West, hoping to resist long enough to allow for outside assistance. That feature of Swedish security policy was buttressed by Danish and Norwegian membership in NATO and further strengthened by the allied deployment plans in the event of war with the Warsaw Pact. Even when by the late 1960s Stockholm moved to affirm neutrality as the centerpiece of its policy, it continued to depend strategically on the West. Finally, Swedish military planning during the Cold War assumed that although Finland was constrained in its ability to pursue an independent foreign and security policy, it remained nonetheless Sweden's frontline state and its first line of defense against the Soviet Union.

Sweden's neutrality evolved into an official ideology tied to the country's domestic politics, especially during and after Olof Palme's prime ministry, but it was often divorced from the region's geostrategic realities and Sweden's overall security position. By the 1970s the ideology of neutrality had become part of Swedish national identity, along with the government's forward position on supporting—albeit in a rather selective way—international institutions and human rights. During the Cold War there was disconnect between Sweden's official opposition to NATO's plans to modernize its nuclear weapons and to nuclear deterrence in general and the country's continued— if indirect—de facto reliance for its own security on NATO's viability and strength.

The tradition of neutrality in Sweden's security policy by itself does not explain why Stockholm did not seek to build a regional defense system after the war. Although Finland was by definition locked out of any regional security negotiations, talks between Sweden, Norway, and Denmark on security cooperation lasted through 1949. Although they did not generate a treaty, the three countries highlighted the shared geostrategic dilemma of all Scandinavians.[2] More important, while Sweden advocated the idea of a regional solution to the Nordic security dilemma, Denmark and Norway remained reluctant and ultimately opted for NATO membership. Perhaps history played a decisive role in that case, as both Denmark and Norway had experienced Nazi occupation during World War II, while Sweden had managed to stay outside the conflict. Although the historical explanation can be pushed too far, it should not be overlooked. It does make a difference that the last time Sweden was involved in a war was in 1814, when it seized Norway from Denmark. The history lesson still very vivid to Swedes is that their brand of neutrality has worked. What made Sweden's policy of neutrality during the Cold War different, especially when compared to that of Finland or Austria, was that it was not built on international agreements but rather was generated internally. In contrast, the Cold War imposed neutrality on Finland and Austria through treaty and meant the foreclosure of alignment as a security policy option. Hence, Swedish neutrality was not only legitimate as an autonomous policy choice but also quintessentially unilateralist in its origin.

In the 1950s and 1960s Sweden continued to invest in national defense capabilities as the essential condition of military nonalignment. The commitment to a strong military reflected genuine Swedish concern that the Soviets might attempt to expand farther to the north to dominate the Baltic littoral. The renewed sense of urgency compelled Stockholm to open secret channels to NATO in the 1950s, relying on Oslo as the conduit. Although until the end of the Cold War Swedish security policy was officially committed to nonalignment in times of peace, with a view to remaining neutral in the event of war, in practice the policy reflected the realization that in the event of a NATO–Warsaw Pact conflict, Sweden would not be able to remain neutral.

The end of the Cold War marked a significant change in Sweden's views on the meaning of its traditional military nonalignment. It brought to the fore the realization that in many respects the Cold War definition of Swedish neutrality was a political fiction, albeit one that had resonated strongly with the Swedish public. The first sign of change and first attempt to adjust Swedish security policy to the post–Cold War environment came during the prime ministry of Carl Bildt, who reformulated Swedish neutrality as "nonparticipation in military alliances, with the aim of making it possible for our country to remain neutral in the event of war in our vicinity."[3] The rationale for Bildt's redefinition was reportedly the result of war games showing that in some conflicts Sweden might not be able to remain neutral. Moreover, at the time there was a growing realization that multilateralism had inherent limits. Even though Sweden's commitment to multilateralism within the United Nations had remained strong, as manifest most visibly by the governments of Olof Palme (1969–1976 and 1982–1986), one could argue that, paradoxically, the policy was unilateralist at the core in that Sweden's neutrality was a precondition for the country's participation in UN peacekeeping missions. In historical perspective, neutrality as practiced by Sweden never prevented Stockholm from becoming an active and assertive participant in various international causes, such as decolonization, the abolition of apartheid in South Africa, or providing developmental aid to Third World countries. While in the area of military security Stockholm insisted on its traditional policy of nonalignment, this was hardly synonymous with nonparticipation in international relations. For instance, in 1982 Olof Palme made Sweden an active international advocate of disarmament.

The decision to join the European Union would prove the most radical redefinition of Swedish security identity—a process still far from complete. During the Cold War Sweden mixed de facto insistence on maximum sovereignty through its own brand of unilateralism with an active multilateral agenda steeped in left-wing politics on the world scene. Sweden's membership in the EC in the 1970s fell victim to the belief that neutrality was central to its security. It took two compelling developments to change the government's position: the severity of Sweden's economic crisis and the collapse of the Berlin Wall. In July 1991 Prime Minister Ingvar Carlsson submitted Sweden's application for EC membership. The November 1994 referendum yielded a narrow majority in favor, and in January 1995, Sweden, along with Finland and Austria, joined the European Union. Norway stayed outside by voting "no" in its referendum to join the European Union. But ever since then, the historical pull of military nonalignment has had an impact on Sweden's security policy.

POST–COLD WAR CONTEXT: NATO, THE EU, AND RUSSIA

An indication of a sea change under way in Swedish foreign and security policy in the 1990s was the government's decision to stop referring to the "policy of neutrality," modifying it instead with the expression "nonparticipation in military alliances." Since the 1990s Sweden has become involved in security and defense cooperation both regionally and globally to a much greater degree than during the Cold War. Most significant is that, as a member of NATO's Partnership for Peace and the Euro-Atlantic Partnership Council, Stockholm has come closer to NATO than at any time before and has done so in a much more open fashion. Although Sweden has stopped short of making formal application to join NATO, it has contributed peacekeepers to Bosnia-Herzegovina and Kosovo in the aftermath of NATO operations. Those were important decisions, especially in light of low levels of public support for Sweden's membership in NATO.[4] The central government's concern was not only the limited support for NATO membership but also the fact that NATO membership would require extending a reciprocal security guarantee under Article 5.

Sweden's ambivalence about NATO membership is likely to persist. In 2003 Sweden's Psychological Defense Agency published a poll showing that only 22 percent of Swedes believed the country should join NATO, 56 percent believed it should remain nonaligned, and 19 percent had no opinion. Interestingly enough and in line with Sweden's tradition of military nonalignment, the same poll showed considerable ambivalence on EU's common defense, with only 15 percent strongly in favor, 24 percent in favor, 27 percent unsure, 12 percent against, 14 percent strongly against, and 7 percent expressing no opinion. Finally, the poll reaffirmed public support for continued strong national defense, with 57 percent "absolutely" in favor, 25 percent in favor, 13 percent unsure, 2 percent against it, and 3 percent having no opinion.[5] Anti-NATO sentiment grew stronger after the 2003 Iraq war. A poll conducted by *Svenska Dagbladet* in January 2004 found that 59 percent of the Swedish public was against joining NATO, with 24 percent in favor.[6]

Sweden's membership in NATO is clearly not in the cards. The majority of the Swedish public is opposed to it, as are most of the political parties. With the exception of the small Liberal Party and three of the Stockholm dailies, there is little popular or government support for the idea of NATO membership. In the 1990s, successive Swedish governments argued that the country's tradition of being militarily nonaligned enhances Sweden's independence and enables it to push vigorously for nuclear disarmament without being constrained by alliance policy. According to a poll conducted by the SOM Institute, published in May 2004 in Sweden's largest daily, 44 percent of Swedes believed the country should not join NATO, with 22 percent in favor of membership, and 34 percent with no opinion on the matter.[7]

Short of NATO membership, Stockholm has focused on redefining the country's security policy. In 1998 the Swedish Defense Commission issued a new threat assessment arguing that the disappearance of the risk of Russian invasion has substantially reduced the need for territorial defense—long the mainstay of Swedish security policy.[8] Since 1999 Stockholm has implemented massive cuts in the Swedish Armed Forces and the country's entire defense system, chiefly as a result of the disappearance of Soviet threat. Still, Sweden remains aware that the long-term direction of Russia's political evolution is uncertain, and residual concerns about the Baltic-Nordic region's security remain. For that reason, in addition to maintaining its residual defense capability, Stockholm has tried to bring Russia into greater cooperation, both bilaterally and on a regional basis. In October 1999 the government published *Russia—A Part of Europe: Swedish Proposals for and EU Policy on Cooperation with Russia*, outlining a blueprint for political and economic engagement with Moscow. It reflected Stockholm's view that the new threats would come in the areas of international terrorism, crime, immigration, and other "soft" security issues, especially as a result of the "welfare wall" between the affluent Scandinavian states and their neighbors to the east.

Although the region's security environment after the Cold War has been benign, Sweden's security is still determined first and foremost by its geostrategic location in northern Europe and its proximity to Russia. While in the past Sweden's security policy emphasized military balance and the country's desire to stay outside superpower competition, Sweden has since the Cold War focused on multilateral regional cooperative agreements. These include the Nordic Council and the Nordic Council of Ministers, the Council of the Baltic Sea States (CBSS), and the Barents Euro-Arctic Council (BEAC). All these are elements of "soft" security cooperation, as they provide a forum for contact and debate.

Another aspect of Sweden's regional security policy has been assistance to the newly independent Baltic states. Every Swedish government since 1991 has made contributing aid to Estonia, Latvia, and Lithuania a priority of Swedish foreign policy. It has included the so-called "sovereignty programs" in civil areas, as well as Swedish assistance to the Baltic states in building up their own military forces, civil defense, coast guard systems, and border control.[9] Although Sweden has opted to remain outside of NATO, it has supported the Baltic states' applications for membership in both NATO and the European Union. Moreover, changes in the Baltic security environment, especially the dramatically improved security along Sweden's southern border, have led to greater involvement in Central Europe. Since 1991 Sweden has expanded engagement with Poland, mainly in the areas of trade and economic cooperation. In 1999 the Swedish government launched an official campaign "Sweden-Poland: Baltic Sea Neighbors in the New Europe," aimed at strengthening Swedish-Polish cooperation.

The lack of support for NATO membership is not the only area where traditional Swedish attitudes continue to dominate. Although Sweden has become a member of the European Union, it remains ambivalent about the scope of integration. For instance, while Finland has joined the European Monetary Union (EMU), yet another referendum on the euro failed in Sweden in 2003, notwithstanding the expected "solidarity vote" in the aftermath of the murder of Sweden's foreign minister Anna Lindh, a strong supporter of the pro-euro campaign. Finland has also appeared more willing to cooperate with NATO, despite pervasive Finnish skepticism about actual membership. Finland's nonalignment was a historical necessity and the only way it could maintain control over its domestic affairs. Conversely, integration in the EU, as well as much greater engagement in NATO than is the Swedish case, reflects Finland's adaptation to a historic opportunity that presented itself after the Soviet Union collapsed.

The two historically different paths to nonalignment that Sweden and Finland traveled during the Cold War undergird the fundamental difference between the two neutrality policies: In the Swedish case it was nonalignment by choice; in the Finnish case it was nonalignment of necessity. Both countries, irrespective of their historical paths, have generated strongly held beliefs and patterns in foreign- and security-policy making. Today Finland remains conditioned to define security in substantive military terms, with an emphasis on defense, while Sweden puts first priority on the civic dimension of security.

SWEDEN'S NATIONAL SECURITY DOCTRINE AND MILITARY REFORM

The post–Cold War environment has offered Sweden unprecedented security from great-power attack, but it has also raised a host of new issues, among them cross-border security and regional security and stability challenges. In 2002 Sweden adopted a new security doctrine, which, although it maintains the country's military nonalignment, no longer centers on neutrality in the event of a conflict in the country's vicinity. The new strategy is tied to a series of studies by the Permanent Defense Commission (*Försvarsberedningen*), established when Sweden joined the EU in 1995 to facilitate discussion between the government and the political parties in the Parliament on how EU membership would affect the nation's security. The Commission published its first report in 1995 and has continued with periodic assessments of the new security environment, emphasizing the progressive "Europeanization" of Swedish security policy.

One of the more proactive regional aspects of current Swedish security-policy reform has been its endorsement of the Baltic states' aspirations to join the EU and NATO as the necessary precondition for regional security and stability. Stockholm has argued that the process of overcoming the divisions of the Cold War era will not be complete until "these countries have also achieved their security policy objectives."[10] Sweden has argued that military reform must be set in the context of relations with NATO, the EU, and Russia. The government considers multilateralism key to regional and global security, and Sweden has insisted that, notwithstanding preponderant American power, the international system is not unipolar and Washington is not in a position to dictate to Europe on such core issues as, for example, missile defense.

The underlying premise of the reconceptualization of Swedish security policy is that while the country faces no threat of invasion in the foreseeable future and can respond to any such threats through the residual deterrent and defensive capabilities of its armed forces, it must nevertheless be ready for future regional or local military conflicts. The Commission's recommendation to amend the law to enable the government to make Swedish forces available for EU–authorized peacekeeping missions abroad without permission from the Riksdag (Parliament) was a significant departure from traditional Swedish security policy in the direction of "Europeanizing" the country. That concession has been offset by the Commission's assertion that since Sweden was not part of a military alliance, it would retain the necessary flexibility to act on its own if the changing regional security environment so required.

The current cycle of Swedish defense reform began in 1999.[11] The present two-year program will run from 2005 through 2007. It seeks to adapt the Swedish military to the new range of security threats, including regional conflict, failing states, weapons proliferation, organized crime, and terrorism. The program reaffirms Sweden's commitment to contributing military personnel to UN peacekeeping operations. It also reaffirms the centrality of the EU to Swedish defense policy, recognizing the continued importance of NATO as the most important forum for cooperation between the United States and Europe and of Sweden's participation in NATO's Partnership for Peace (PfP) program, a defense cooperation program established in 1994 aimed at greater interoperability and dialogue between NATO and Partner countries.

The defense budget, set for 2005 at SEK38.65[12] billion will sustain mainly the operational forces, leading to further reductions and decommissioning of units. The draft requirements for the Swedish armed forces, specified in the Defense Commission's 2004 report *Defense for a New Time*, includes recommendations for a SEK3 billion reduction in the defense budget, to be fully implemented in 2007, and provisions for Sweden's contributing to the EU's rapid reaction capability.[13] In addition to Sweden's participation in the European Rapid Reaction Force (ERRF), defense reform proposals for 2005 call for further technological transformation of the Swedish armed forces in the direction of net-centric or network-based defense (NBD). The reform program also calls for changes in the way conscripts are trained, so as to provide for between eight thousand and ten thousand conscripts per year for the duration of the 2005–2007 program. While Sweden will preserve conscription and the tradition of national military service, it will place greater emphasis on the professional and voluntary component of its forces. Conscript training will run for eleven months (divided into two terms), with an optional three to five months of specialized training for units preparing to deploy for international missions. The new system for the training of draftees should be in place by 2006.

Today Sweden is in the midst of its most extensive military reform ever. Sweden's extensive Cold War–era defense establishment needs to be replaced with a flexible operational defense system. Needless to say, because of the very size of its residual military, the task Sweden faces is far more daunting than that of any other Scandinavian country. The reform will radically decrease the size of and restructure the Swedish armed forces. As of February 2005 the total strength of the Swedish armed forces was approximately 37 thousand.[14] The armed forces will continue to downsize, with a 25-percent reduction planned between 2005 and 2007. The goal is to retire senior officers in order to increase the overall pool of younger officers, between twenty and forty years of age, who are deemed critical for the planned operational defense. Sweden also wants to leverage its traditional niches in equipment, especially in network-based command-and-control systems, aircraft, and combat vehicles. It is an urgent problem, for reductions in Swedish defense spending have decreased procurement and thus had an impact on the country's defense sector. Throughout the 1990s and into the 2000s Sweden's defense industry struggled to remain viable, despite the growing integration and cooperation with other countries, in particular the United Kingdom. For example, the record of sales for the current generation of the JAS Gripen multipurpose aircraft has been mixed.

The dramatic changes in global security in the wake of the September 11 terrorist attack on the United States compelled the Defense Commission to revisit Sweden's overall security situation.[15] EU enlargement in particular pushed Swedish security optics further south and east, as it began to adapt to the upcoming EU membership for Poland, Estonia, Latvia, and Lithuania. Sweden may soon recognize that when it comes to security policy it is not only the north that is important but also Europe as a whole. Some steps in that direction have already been taken. Like Finland, Sweden supports implementation of the so-called 1992 Petersberg Tasks, including EU military deployments for peacekeeping, crisis management, and humanitarian assistance, but it also realizes that it needs to maintain a capability to deal with possible combat issues outside the immediate periphery.

The Balkan experience, especially the lessons of NATO's Kosovo campaign, made it clear that the EU needed to upgrade its capabilities if it were to present a meaningful alternative to NATO. The experience of the 2001 campaign in Afghanistan and the 2003 war in Iraq further strengthened the realization that without real capabilities improvement, the EU would be unable to offer Sweden a viable alternative to its traditional reliance on nonalignment and its own defense spending to provide for the country's security.

THE LEGACY OF FINNISH NEUTRALITY AND POST–COLD WAR SECURITY POLICY

During the Cold War, Finland's position on neutrality was quite different from that of her larger neighbor to the northwest. Unlike Sweden, Finland emerged from World War II as a combatant state, first defeated by the Soviet Union in the Winter War of 1940, then aligned with Germany, and yet again rendered defenseless vis-à-vis the Soviet Union in the wake of the armistice of 1944. At the end of the war, Finland found itself effectively in the Soviet sphere of influence and was compelled to enter into a Treaty of Friendship and Mutual Assistance with Moscow. Until 1991 Finland's foreign and security policy would recognize Soviet strategic prerogative in the Baltic region, including the limitations on Finland's armed forces. Helsinki's room to maneuver on foreign and security policy would be circumscribed by its relations with Moscow for the duration of the Cold War. Finland's "neutrality" during that time lacked the added ideological element of identity inherent in the Swedish experience.

Finland's territorial defense and the conscription-based army that it maintained during the Cold War offered the country a degree of defense capability and some deterrence, the latter in light of the Finnish forces' performance record during the 1940 Winter War. However, Finland's military capabilities remained marginal in the context of NATO–Warsaw Pact competition, especially considering the degree of Finland's geostrategic vulnerability and her limited resources. Finland's dependence on Soviet goodwill was poignantly underscored by the presence of a Soviet military base on Finnish territory, which was returned to Finnish control only in 1955—more than a decade after the conclusion of hostilities. More important, throughout the Cold War Moscow repeatedly indicated that it did not recognize Finland as neutral but in fact saw it as part of its sphere of influence.

Living in the shadow of Soviet military power, neutrality would acquire for Finland a far more immediate significance than the more ideologically laden Swedish view. It was inextricably intertwined with determination to retain sovereignty on domestic issues and thus to preserve the country's democratic institutions. The end of the Cold War made military alignment a viable option for Finland for the first time since World War II. Finland's EU membership, accompanied by the enlargement of NATO and the European Union into postcommunist Europe, has redefined the geostrategic context that Finland inhabits today. Even though Finland continues to be a part of the European Union's new boundary, for the first time it has been able to overcome its peripheral position on the map of democratic Europe, becoming instead firmly embedded in European security architecture.

The end of the Cold War revolutionized Finland's security in another way as well. Not unlike Germany, Finland has regained full sovereignty over its foreign- and security-policy making, and whatever concessions it will make from now on will be arrived at through autonomous national decision-making processes. As one scholar put it, the end of the Cold War opened up for Finland the possibility of a "new identity formation" in the area of national security.[16] The quest has proceeded in three directions, as Finland has remained engaged with the Organization for Security and Cooperation in Europe (OSCE), joined the European Union, and cooperated with NATO while choosing to remain outside the alliance. In Finland, the levels of public support for NATO membership are even lower than in Sweden. A poll measuring Finnish support levels published in February 2004 showed 22 percent in favor, 56 percent against, and 22 percent with no opinion.[17] Those figures looked even weaker when considered in light of how the public ranked the most effective defense policy for the future. A poll published in June 2004 showed that 57 percent of Finns supported maintaining strong national defense, that 23 percent supported transforming the EU into an effective defensive alliance, and that only 12 percent opted for joining NATO. Eight percent were undecided.[18]

Finland has also had a special interest in promoting good relations with Russia as a means of enhancing its own security and the security of Northern

Europe as a whole. Finland's post–Cold War security policy emerged at the intersection of the European Union, NATO, and Russia/Northern Europe. Helsinki's decision to look to the EU as its primary security framework is in part a result of history. Finland never had the same capability as Sweden did to base its defense strategy on its own power, and even though the post–Cold War security environment is benign, Finland remains geostrategically exposed. That is why after the Cold War Helsinki initially looked for multilateral security options, first from the Conference for Security and Cooperation in Europe (forerunner of the OSCE) as it appeared to be the only available formula for enhancing cooperative security, while the country remained committed to its traditional territorial defense. In the end, Finland would frame its national-security policy choices in the multilateralism of the European Union structures, set against the larger UN context as the source of global legitimacy.

EU membership has become Finland's preferred anchor in Europe, as it offers assurances against the marginalization of the country. Finland formally applied for EU membership in 1992—the decision driven in part by Sweden's application a year earlier but also by the important security dimension based on the anticipated future transformation of the EU.[19] The referendum on membership, notwithstanding the rather limited debate that accompanied it, can be viewed as the beginning of Finland's proactive security policy. Finland's EU membership completes the country's self-identification with Europe, decisively ending the "special status" it had maintained during the Cold War on account of its geostrategic position. In symbolic terms, the end of the Cold War and EU membership marked the "normalization" of Finland's security policy. Perhaps it is significant that EU membership contains an indirect "existential" security guarantee that allowed Finland to gradually shift away from its Cold War status.

As a small state in the EU, Finland must find a formula for ensuring that its voice will be recognized in Brussels, especially on matters of national security. The attendant question then is the extent to which Helsinki would commit itself to explicit reciprocal security-treaty arrangements. Those two issues have been central to the evolution of Finland's security policy. An answer to the first question would come in Finland's support for the European Union's Common Foreign and Security Policy (CFSP). The CFSP allowed Finland to engage in European security issues without undertaking the explicit Article 5–type treaty commitments that NATO membership requires. Moreover, the intergovernmental nature of the CFSP, its consensus provision, and its regional (European) dimension would prove strong selling points for the Finns. Even more important was the possibility of opting out of individual decisions and the ability for small states like Finland to take refuge in the unanimity rule.

For Finland, participation in the CFSP and, subsequently, the ESDP marked the clear national preference for the EU over NATO. The EU option seemed to represent an intermediate step in the evolution of Finnish security policy between forced nonalignment of the Cold War era on the one hand, and full alignment required by NATO membership on the other hand. The EU option also emphasized the political rather than strictly military aspect of the security arrangement. It enabled Finland to develop strong multilateral political ties within the EU while maintaining its strong traditional commitment to national territorial defense and conscription. In strictly military terms, Finland has maintained an arm's-length approach to alliances—more so toward NATO than the EU—while preserving the foundations of its national defense identity. Although Finland was the first among the former neutrals to become an observer with the North Atlantic Cooperation Council (NACC) and become a member of the PfP, it has been explicit from the start that—unlike the post-communist democracies—it did not consider those actions as steps to NATO membership. Finland seems to have joined the EU with the implicit expectation that should membership entail common defense, Finland would eventually participate fully in such provisions. But the conditions under which Finland joined the EU suggest that the country preferred to do so gradually, first coordinating with the EU in crisis-management tasks.

Russia has remained the principal security concern for Finland, much more than has been the case for Sweden. Following the emergence of the Russian Federation, concerns centered on conventional threats to Northern Europe, as well as crime, border-control issues, and terrorism. Finland has emphasized the need to maintain stable defense capability, while at the same time it has sought to serve as an intermediary between Russia and the European Union. The current benign security environment has given Finland unprecedented policy flexibility. Helsinki has offered assistance to the newly independent Baltic States as part of its regional engagement with an eye to multilateral cooperative security in the North. While Finland's relations with Russia have been the most open to date, Helsinki's policy toward Moscow can be described as one of high alertness, if not suspicion, about the future direction of policy of its most important Eastern neighbor. Membership in the EU has enabled Finland to make conditionality in relations with Russia a viable principle without appearing to pressure Russia unilaterally. Russia's greater acceptance of the EU on its periphery, as opposed to its often strenuous objections to NATO enlargement into the Baltic area, has made that task all the more easy.

For Finland, EU membership offers the prospect of relying on the ESDP while also preserving the country's flexibility on national security policy. In contrast, NATO membership today would constrain its policy options while offering limited benefits in the current security environment. The regional orientation, combined with its membership in the European Union has made Finland into a poor candidate for the new "expeditionary" vision of NATO. Today Finish security policy combines a small state's traditional calculus of military security with an emphasis on multilateral political arrangements and conditionality. The overarching goal is to seek security through a wider regional and all-European political and economic integration. Finland sees itself first in Europe, with transatlanticism taking a distinctly second place. At the same time, the post–Cold War progressive "Europeanization" of Finland must always be weighed against the country's Russian policy: On the one hand, Helsinki has aligned its policy with that of the European Union; on the other hand, it has sought to impress on Brussels the special challenge Russia presents to the Baltic-Nordic subregion.

Finland's bet is that, should conditions in the east deteriorate, its membership in the EU will have a deterrent and preventive effect when it comes to relations with Russia. That is one of the reasons Finland supported EU membership for the Baltic states and initiated what the EU terms its Northern Dimension, to ensure that EU impact on the Baltic-Nordic subregion would become more pronounced. Finland's goal was to make the newly emergent region an integral part of Europe after 2004.

The Finns do not believe that staying outside NATO makes them free riders. Finland's position is that by maintaining credible defense, in combination with EU membership and participation in EU crisis-management tasks, it is contributing to regional security. It remains to be seen how Finland will respond in the event the ESDP develops meaningful military options. Moreover, while it remains outside NATO, Finland has strengthened its cooperation with the alliance through the PfP and the enhanced PfP. Cooperation with NATO has also benefited the Finnish armaments industry, contributing to greater compatibility of Finland's military with NATO forces and strengthening the "socializing" effect of cooperation. In the longer term, Helsinki should be able to field a brigade-size force for international tasks.

Finnish thinking about national security and the ultimate value of alliance has remained tied to the experience of the Winter War, when Finland learned firsthand the importance of self-reliance. Today the Finns maintain the view that ultimately only strong national defense can offer some assurance to a small state. Conversely, if NATO membership does not offer Finland significant added security value, its out-of-area focus would detract from the state's primary defensive task. That view may change depending on future developments in Russia, but in the final analysis, Finland sees the EU as better fitting its security needs and strategy, while at the same time viewing both the EU and NATO as complementary solutions. The key question is how Helsinki will adapt when the EU introduces meaningful common defense.

That would likely induce Finland to reassess its traditional emphasis on independent defense, though change in defense identity would also likely be cushioned by a record of involvement with the ESDP.

This gradual process of adaptation is already on the way. A government report entitled *Finnish Security and Defense Policy 2004* published by the Prime Minister's Office in September 2004 made the development of the EU's security and defense capabilities Finland's number-one security-policy priority, with NATO and transatlantic relations a close second. The EU focus of Finland's security policy has added focus on regional issues, including the issue of combating terrorism. The report has emphasized that it is "crucial to increase bilateral and multilateral cooperation in neighborhood relations, regionally and globally, and establish procedures that are legally binding."[20] To complete the gamut of its options, Finland has reaffirmed its insistence that decisions on the use of military power must be made in the multilateral context and under the mandate of the United Nations.

FINNISH DEFENSE REFORM

For Finland, Northern Europe remains the principal regional focus of security policy, and it sets the context for its counterterrorism capabilities within the EU. Here the emphasis is on greater internal security and police capabilities and enhanced capabilities to investigate international terrorist threats, exchange intelligence information, and share analysis. The 2004 report on Finnish security policy reaffirmed the country's commitment to nonalignment, buttressed by its historical preference for territorial defense. In addition, Finland will remain committed to the development of a voluntary national defense force. It expects to have the army's readiness brigades fully operational in 2008, with enhanced firepower and mobility.

Beginning in 2009, Finland plans to increase ground-based air defense and regional defense forces, as well as develop the navy's ability to protect the sea lines, improve mine countermeasures, and deploy mobile coastal-defense units. In addition, the air force will undergo a midcycle update to the Hornet, its mainstay aircraft, including the acquisition of long-range precision-guided weapons for air-to-surface operations.[21] At the same time, the Finnish army will be modernized with Leopard 2 tanks, CV-9030 armored fighting vehicles, new antitank missiles, and heavy rocket launchers to give it the capability to strike in-depth enemy targets.

In 2004 Finland's peacetime active duty armed forces stood at approximately 27,000 personnel.[22] The current Finnish defense reform program stipulates that in 2008 the total mobilized wartime strength of the army will be set at 285,000, with 60,000 operational troops and 225,000 regional troops; the total size of the navy is projected at 30,000 personnel in 2008, including both naval units and coastal troops. The air force will fly 63 F/A-18 Hornets, with transport and liaison aircraft scheduled for replacement in 2010. After 2009 the Finnish army will concentrate on developing ground-based air defenses and strengthening regional defense forces.[23] Like Denmark, Finland is also framing its reforms in terms of generating "total defense," combining military and civil-defense tasks. Overall, Finland is maintaining a sizable military establishment, especially when one considers its population is only over 5 million.

The 2004 dual NATO/EU enlargement transformed Finland's regional security optics, making the Baltic Sea a "joint inland sea of the EU and Russia."[24] Finland's security policy, its defense reform, and its regional concerns are driven by the decision to remain outside NATO, by the proximity of the Russian Federation, and by the strong sense that Finland has become a "frontier state" of the European Union. Today Finland's policy is also more sensitive to regional security concerns—not just in the Baltic-Nordic region but also in Central Europe. The Finnish government has recognized that EU enlargement has made Poland and Germany Finland's neighbors and "increasingly important partners"[25] in the EU. Finland also recognizes that current problems in the region are not only the traditional security concerns but also those connected to environmental, maritime, and nuclear safety, as well as organized crime and terrorism.

Finland has invested additional resources to enhance the Finnish Security Police (*Suojelupoliisi*, or Supo), especially in the area of terrorism prevention. In Finland's counterterrorist strategy, intelligence sharing has become the centerpiece of Supo's new strategy, especially bilateral intelligence cooperation. Finland's focus has been on terrorism prevention, including the establishment of a special terrorism-prevention unit in Supo in 2003.[26] In addition to enhancing airport, maritime, and transit security (though the government stopped short of introducing sky marshals on commercial flights), Finland introduced a new chapter into its criminal code directed against terrorism, which became effective on February 1, 2003. Muslim extremism has not been an urgent issue in Finland—certainly nothing compared to the experience of Denmark, Sweden, or Continental Europe generally—as historically Finland has had low levels of immigration. However, membership in the European Union has made the problem of Islamic radicalism bred in Europe an important concern of Finland's police and security forces. All counterterrorist policies pursued by the Finns are in the context of EU counterterrorist initiatives—part of an effort to strike a balance between Finland's traditional concept of defense and EU requirements.

In addition to preserving credible national defense, Finland has been moving slowly into areas of international operations, with the goal of striking a balance between the two. The Finnish government views combating terrorism as part of combating organized crime in general. Finland has supported the EU initiatives to implement counterterrorism conventions and has committed to participating within the EU framework in operations to assist developing countries in combating terrorism on their territory. It has also assisted in EU efforts to prevent proliferation of WMD and to eliminate sources of terrorist financing.

The 2004 defense policy statement shows that Finland remains determined to build its defense strategy on two fundamental pillars: indigenous territorial defense and participation in the ESDP, to be buttressed by close cooperation with NATO but short of membership, and working for a global multilateral UN–dominated security regime. Though Finland supports strong transatlantic ties, it considers EU unity to be vital when it comes to relations with the United States, and the European Union takes precedence over transatlanticism.

FINLAND AND THE NORTHERN DIMENSION

Finland launched its most significant attempt to engage Russia within the larger EU context. The so-called Northern Dimension idea was put forth immediately after Sweden and Finland joined the European Union. Russia then became the next-door neighbor of the EU, and its importance has grown even more since the three Baltic states and Poland joined the EU in 2004. The European Council meeting in Luxembourg in December 1997 asked the European Commission to examine Finland's initiative. In turn, the European Commission recommended that the Northern Dimension be made part of the EU's external relations. The idea is built on the premise of geographically bringing together the countries of the Council of the Baltic Sea States and the Barents Euro-Arctic Council, while the EU builds on a set of existing relationships with the members of both organizations. In effect, the Northern Dimension is a mirror image of the EU's relations with Mediterranean countries. The initiative was drafted with an eye on integration and economic cooperation.

The combined territory of the nine countries bordering on the Baltic Sea is bigger than Europe. Their combined population is almost 300 million, and the region offers opportunities for investment and international business in the Baltic area. There is also a security dimension to the initiative. The Baltic Sea and the St. Petersburg regions are the traditional route to the Russian heartland, while Finland and the three Baltic states can serve as the doors to trade in western Russia. The proposed projects include more harbors, better internal routes, telecommunications, dealing with environmental degradation and unsafe nuclear reactors in the St. Petersburg area and Lithuania and curbing emissions and pollution of the Baltic Sea.

Two issues that constitute serious security concerns in Scandinavia and the Baltic region in the fallout from September 11 are illegal immigration and organized crime, both of which have acquired new urgency in light of the threat of international terrorism. In order to address these problems, close cooperation with Russia will be essential.

Energy security is another important consideration for the region. Since the EU will be increasingly dependent on imported energy, Russia will remain a vital economic partner for the EU, especially in the area of natural gas imports. Russia has one-third of all the world's known reserves of natural gas, most of which are in the northern Ural Mountains and the Barents Sea, and the most important area of economic cooperation between Russia and the EU will focus on tapping those gas reserves. The use of new gas reserves will require the construction of new pipelines and offshore installations for transporting gas from Russia to the EU.

Structured as an array of projects that will last for decades, the Northern Dimension offers the Nordic states a promising framework for economic cooperation with Russia. Administratively, the Northern Dimension will rest on the Council of the Baltic Sea States (CBSS) and the Barents Euro-Arctic Council (BEAC). Funding will come from the EU's Tacis and Phare programs, two EU assistance initiatives to postcommunist states in the region, as well as from private investment. But economic cooperation is but one aspect of the initiative. Russia's western border remains one of the world's most important geopolitical frontiers. The Northern Dimension wants to reach across that frontier, tying economic development to security for both sides. As for the significance of the initiative on the regional level, suffice it to say that the Finns at times compare the Northern Dimension to the European integration initiative after the Second World War.

DENMARK AND THE LEGACY OF ATLANTICISM

Denmark is a small state that has been an active member of NATO, as well as a member of the European Union with the opt-out on common foreign and defense policy. Historical considerations and Denmark's geostrategic position make it imperative for that country to rely on allied defense to provide for its security. The legacy of the Second World War and the experience of the Cold War made Denmark into one of the staunchest proponents of transatlantic security, continued strong engagement with the United States, and rebuilding the transatlantic relationship after the 2003 rift over Iraq. Denmark's security obligations stretch outside Europe. In addition to Denmark proper, the Kingdom of Denmark includes Greenland—the world's largest island—and the Faroe Islands situated in the middle of the North Atlantic, of which seventeen out of the total eighteen are inhabited. The scope of Denmark's security commitments in terms of sheer territory makes clear that the country lacks the requisite indigenous resources to pursue a credible security strategy on its own.

Territorial defense is still an important goal, but overall Denmark's security policy has been moving in new directions.[27] After 1989 the Danish forces were restructured away from the primary task of territorial defense and toward the direction of crisis management and international defense in the framework of NATO, UN, or OSCE; NATO remains the centerpiece of Danish security policy. Since the end of the Cold War, Denmark's relations within NATO have become more harmonious than at any time prior to that. During the Cold War Denmark was at times out of step with NATO over issues of aircraft basing and nuclear weapons,[28] but since 1991 it has become a proactive participant in NATO missions and a strong supporter of alliance outreach and enlargement. For example, Denmark participated in the Kosovo operation with a preponderant parliamentary vote of support and with the support of all centrist parties in the Danish parliament.

Denmark's position on the defense dimension of the EU has been defined by the so-called national compromise of 1992, whereby Denmark chose to remain outside the defense dimension of the EU, including the Western European Union (WEU), common defense policy, and common defense. The Danish opt-out does not imply, however, that the Danes would interfere in the development of closer cooperation in that area by other EU member states. It does, however, underscore that any modification of the opt-out would require a national referendum, which in the current period would most likely fail as the Danish public remains skeptical on the issue.[29]

Danish lack of interest in EU security policy, including the ESDP, has been balanced by extraordinary activism within NATO. Denmark is much more comfortable with the transatlantic dimension of NATO than with the Continental dimension of the EU. The history of German occupation during World War II and the precarious postwar position in the face of Soviet power solidified the view that the NATO alliance and the United States in particular hold the key to Danish security.[30] Paradoxically, Denmark's strong transatlanticism may also suggest that the Danes consider the risk of being constrained by the EU to be higher than constraint by NATO.

Among the old NATO allies Denmark has stood the closest to the United States in Iraq. The pro–American policy is arguably more a function of Denmark's being a small power in the region than an overwhelming commitment to U.S. objectives in the Middle East. Still, the Danish public has seemed more in tune with U.S. policy than the majority of the European public has been. A "Eurobarometer" survey released in November 2003, showed that 57 percent of the Danish population believed the war against Iraq was justified. Moreover, Denmark was the only country in the EU at the time in which the majority of the population supported the Iraq war. In contrast, two-thirds of all EU citizens considered the 2003 Iraq war unjustified.[31] Finally, the same poll showed that 77 percent of Danes were in favor of sending national troops, and 76 percent were willing to contribute to the reconstruction of Iraq. Those figures were well above the average 50 percent for the countries of the European Union as a whole.

Denmark has also been ahead of the other Scandinavians in its direct support for the U.S. strategy of Global War on Terrorism (GWOT). In October 2003 the Danes sent a C-130 with seventy-seven crew and support personnel to Iraq, as well as four F-16s with pilots from the Danish Air Force for air-to-ground operations and support personnel. In addition, approximately 100 Danish Special Operations Forces personnel were deployed under U.S. command, and in Afghanistan the Danes suffered casualties as a part of ISAF operations.[32] Denmark was one of only four countries (Australia, Great Britain, and Poland were the others) to join the United States in sending forces to fight in the first phase of the Iraq war, contributing a small surface warship and a submarine. It is also noteworthy that Copenhagen displayed considerable staying power in Iraq. While the terror attack in Madrid in March 2004 reverberated through the Danish body politic, the impact was lesser in Denmark than in other European countries. Although left-wing opposition called for the withdrawal of the 500 Danish troops serving in Iraq, the Danish government insisted that they would remain.

Danish Prime Minister Anders Fogh Rasmussen remained committed to the transatlantic relationship as the foundation of his country's security policy, notwithstanding the political price the opposition argued he would pay as a result. Rasmussen's popularity dropped significantly in 2004, compared to the high marks he had received for his presidency of the European Union in the second half of 2002 when he concluded the negotiations finalizing the 2004 EU enlargement.[33] Even so, Rasmussen never wavered in his commitment to transatlanticism, calling repeatedly for the rebuilding of U.S.–European relations. Despite criticism from the opposition, on February 8, 2005, Rasmussen won his second term as Denmark's prime minister in an early election convincingly.[34]

DENMARK'S "TOTAL DEFENSE"

Denmark's near-term defense policy will be guided by the so-called Defense Agreement 2005–2009, which reflects the consensus and compromises of the country's political parties on the direction of defense reform. The Agreement speaks of the traditional Danish commitment to the defense of Denmark and its allies, while it emphasizes the need to strengthen Denmark's defense capabilities in two critical areas: "(1) internationally deployable military capabilities, and (2) the ability to counter terror acts and their consequences."[35] Both objectives seem to be closely aligned with NATO's transformation goals and with American objectives in the Global War on Terrorism.

While the Danes support the United Nations agenda, their first priority is collective defense anchored in NATO as "the framework of the transatlantic partnership and a guarantor of European security."[36] This commitment has manifest in Copenhagen's contribution to the NATO Response Force (NRF). Denmark's security policy and its unqualified support for NATO keep open the possibility that, should Denmark remove the opt-out from the EU defense policy, it could also participate in EU peacekeeping missions. That is likely to become an important consideration in the course of Danish defense reform for the next five years, should NATO's capabilities become marginal.

Denmark reacted forcefully to the changed international security environment following the September 11 terrorist attacks against the United States. Because of its historically open immigration policy, Denmark considers terrorist threats to be serious, including those that may not originate within the country or from the immediate proximity to Danish territory. Defining the task as one of "total defense," Danish defense reform has moved away from the conventional conscript training for territorial defense and toward merging and integrating military and national-emergency responders. The current defense agreement calls for changes to Article 81 of the Danish Constitution to permit adjusting conscription requirements with total defense in mind. In addition, the Home Guard is to be integrated into the operational and support structures of Danish Defense.

In 2005 the Danish armed forces numbered approximately 24,000, excluding civilians.[37] The armed forces are still based on the pool of twelve thousand troops required to complete a seven-hundred-hour training program over four months. However, the Danish government and parliament have been reviewing the continued efficacy of the draft-based military, focusing on how to adjust the numbers and duration of service by the end of 2006. That is in part because the defense agreement calls for the reorganization of

Denmark's military forces in order to prepare them for power-projection operations and international missions. In that regard, Copenhagen has committed to generating a force of two thousand (fifteen hundred from the army and five hundred from the navy and the air force) for international operations. At the same time, the Danes will disband the residual mobilization defense system and restructure it to support operational units for total-defense tasks, especially counterterrorism. The Home Guard and the Ministry of Defense will be further integrated under the authority of the defense minister. While some form of conscription will be retained as a means of military recruitment, it will be reformed to meet the requirements of total defense. Overall personnel reductions will be accompanied by qualitative improvements, including some barracks and base closings. Finally, the government has promised to spend additional money to fund greater Danish participation in international operations.[38]

The current Danish reform program will run through 2009. It stipulates the reorganization of the army into two brigades within the Danish Division, integrated and trained for NATO's Response Force (NRF). In an effort to maximize flexibility, the Danish Division will be affiliated both with the Allied Command Europe Rapid Reaction Corps, headquartered in Rheindahlen, Germany, and with the Multinational Corps North East, headquartered in Szczecin, Poland, although there have been discussions of Denmark's pulling out of the Szczecin corps. In addition, Denmark plans to contribute a headquarters company, a reconnaissance unit, a military-police unit, and staff personnel drawn from the army's two brigades to the Multinational Standby Forces High Readiness Brigade (SHIRBRIG) for UN operations. Interestingly enough, the Danes are quite proactive in their view of SHIRBRIG's missions, arguing that they should be taken beyond traditional peacekeeping operations into peacemaking under Chapter VII of the UN Charter.

Re-equipment holds the key to the Danish reform. In order to increase power-projection capability, the Danes plan to purchase new Hercules C130J transport aircraft and new EH 101 helicopters. The updates of the Danish F-16s have been aimed at increasing their deployability outside their national sovereignty defense, especially for NRF missions. From among the forty-eight operational F-16s that will be maintained by the Danish Air Force, sixteen will be designated specifically for NATO missions, with eight of those sixteen maintained at high-readiness levels. In addition, Denmark will designate three transports for NATO missions, one of them at a high-readiness level. Overall, the restructuring of the Danish Air Force suggests that, like Norway, Denmark remains serious about defense reform and adaptation to power-projection NATO missions. As part of the air force restructuring for power-projection missions, Denmark will eliminate its land-based air-defense system (DeHawk) and create an autonomous deployable staff that can be deployed either autonomously or with other Danish units. It appears that the modernization of the air force, especially the F-16 updates, is in part a direct result of NATO's aerial operations during the Kosovo war in 1999, where interoperability of U.S. and non–U.S. NATO allies was an issue that generated concern on the American side.

Danish defense spending will likely remain steady, with increases overall from DKK16.5 billion in 2004 and DKK16.6 billion in 2005, to DKK19.3 billion for 2006 and 2007, and a slight decline to DKK19.2 billion for 2008 and DKK19.1 billion for 2009. However, those generally steady numbers do not tell the whole story about Danish reform, such as the decision to set aside DKK2.843 billion each year for equipment modernization to help narrow the gap between Denmark and the United Kingdom and the United States.[39] In the coming years, the Danes are likely to both remain proactive within NATO and work closely at the regional level, especially in the Baltic region and Central Europe.

NORWEGIAN SECURITY POLICY WITHIN NATO

Alongside Denmark, Norway has remained firmly committed to transatlanticism and NATO; as a country outside the European Union, it continues to emphasize the remaining viability of the alliance and its close association with the United States. At this writing, the Norwegian government is in the process of implementing its current 2002–2005 long-term defense plan. The so-called Long-Term Plan is intended to bring about a comprehensive reorganization and restructuring of Norwegian defense.[40] It calls for augmenting the power-projection capabilities of the Norwegian armed forces, while also bringing about reductions in the size of the Norwegian military.

Evolving from its history of German occupation in World War II and its reliance on NATO during the Cold War, Norway's thinking about security has focused on the Nordic region. Historically, Norway has been the least engaged in the Baltic littoral, especially in comparison to the record of involvement in the region by Sweden, Denmark, or Finland. Swedes, Danes, and Finns have historically displayed a much stronger Baltic identity than Norway, even though Norway never recognized the incorporation of the Baltic states into the Soviet Union. More than other factors, sheer geography has dictated Norway's transatlantic and Nordic security identity. In geostrategic terms, Russia remains today the only military security concern for the Norwegians, as it is the only country in the region with the residual capability to pose a conventional threat to Norway. For that reason, Oslo sees itself as still very much dependent on the support of its allies, with NATO being "the most important guarantee of Norwegian security."[41] The commitment to NATO as the centerpiece of Norway's post–Cold War security has remained strong in the aftermath of 1999 NATO enlargement and the September 11 attack.[42] Norway thinks of itself predominantly as an Atlantic state, and it looks to the United States and NATO as the principal guarantors of security in the North Atlantic. Hence, like Denmark, Norway is committed to defense reform, and it has taken seriously American pressure on NATO members to bring their military capabilities in line with power-projection missions.

The adoption of the Long-Term Plan constitutes an implicit admission on Norway's part that in the first post–Cold War decade, the country's military reform program failed to generate sufficient results. Norway has some lost time to make up when it comes to defense reform. In the 1990s the financial resources allocated to Norwegian operational forces were arguably below the requisite levels. Norway's defense budget for 2005–2008 will total NOK118 billion at 2004 prices, yielding an average annual budget of NOK29.5 billion for the cycle—a slight increase over the 2004 defense spending level.[43] The overall goal of Norway's defense reform is to shift from the pattern of large-scale mobilization to a smaller force, but one with high readiness levels. Because of tight budgets, including the projected cut of Norwegian crown NOK2 billion, the current program will have to accomplish more with less. It calls for reducing personnel by five thousand while restructuring the armed forces for the new power-projection missions. The changes advocated for the Norwegian defense system call for smaller forces but for more new technology. That can be achieved through savings; Norway no longer considers it imperative to be able to mobilize large defense forces in the event of an attack, as had been the case during the Cold War, when the defense of the nation's territory was key.

Oslo recognizes that European security has undergone a radical transformation since 1991, especially following the two rounds of NATO enlargement. While Russia is not perceived as a source of direct threat in the near future and the Norwegians do not anticipate that to change in the coming decade, the Norwegian-Russian relationship will remain asymmetric, as between a small state and a great power, with inherent potential for tension. Norwegian security policy stipulates that the country retain the capability of defending on its own against a small-scale attack on its territory, while it plans to defend against a large-scale attack with assistance from its NATO allies. The country's geostrategic location and its energy reserves make it necessary to combine sufficient territorial and maritime defense capabilities with forces that could meet NATO requirements in the coming years. Preserving NATO viability is Norway's core national security interest. However, Norway also plans to eventually be able to contribute forces to EU and UN missions, as well as to the NATO missions that are its primary focus.

NORWEGIAN DEFENSE REFORM

In order to retain territorial defense capability, Norway remains committed to conscription, both as a means for socializing the different segments of Norwegian society and as a way of selecting specialized personnel for the armed forces. In early 2005 the Norwegian armed forces stood at approximately 27,000.[44] The current reform program for 2005 stipulates that Norway's reformed army consist of two brigades and a mobile divisional command in Inner Troms, plus a number of smaller units, including the King's Guard and the Border Guard Company. The Home Guard will be retained at the level of sixty thousand personnel, and it will be based across the country; it should be subsequently reduced to fifty thousand, with thirty-three thousand reserves. At the same time Norway will reduce the number of Home Guard districts from eighteen to twelve, while retaining their overall district, sector, and area structure.

The Norwegian navy will consist of five Fridtjof Nansen Class frigates carrying helicopters, six submarines, eight minesweepers, and one minelayer. In addition, the coast guard will receive new helicopters and a new patrol vessel, reinforced to operate in ice. The first frigate is scheduled to enter service in 2005. The air force will have forty-eight (plus ten) F-16 combat aircraft deployed in three squadrons, with additional aircraft fitted for electronic-warfare support, maritime patrol aircraft, six transport aircraft, and 18 transport helicopters. Norway's Special Forces (Norwegian Army Special Operations Command), or NORASOC, will be given high priority in resource allocation and development, and it will receive improved transport. The goal is to train for multinational operations within NATO, as identified through NATO's Defense Capabilities Initiative (DCI). Most important, Norway plans to raise the readiness levels of its armed forces significantly.[45]

In a follow-up defense-reform proposal to the Norwegian Parliament, published by the Norwegian Defense Department in March 2004, the government reaffirmed its commitment to the two-track reform, both ensuring the territorial and maritime defense capability on the one hand and transforming the military for participation in power projection missions on the other. In that regard, the Norwegians are following a general pattern of post–Cold War restructuring of their defense system similar to that of the

Danes. The Norwegian plan also includes the creation of an ISTAR unit (intelligence, surveillance, target acquisition, and reconnaissance) for missions within NATO, ready to operate in a multinational setting. In addition, Norway plans for a five-thousand-strong rapid-reaction force within the Home Guard, with twenty-five thousand reinforcement and twenty thousand follow-on forces. Also, in order to increase professionalization, the Norwegian defense department has introduced the new subaltern officer rank (from sergeant to lieutenant), with duties similar to those of regular officers but with contract termination when the subaltern reaches thirty-five years of age. The proposed reform would make it mandatory for a select group of officers to accept postings abroad.

Counterterrorism has become an essential component of Norwegian defense reform. After September 11, Norway put in place several antiterrorist measures, including immediate supplemental funding in 2002 for civil defense, emergency responders, and the police. Additional counterterrorist measures were authorized for the Norwegian Ministry of Justice and the police force. The restructuring of the armed forces aimed at achieving higher levels of readiness and mobility was driven by the heightened concern about international terrorism and the need to have faster response times in case of an attack. Norway's counterterrorism policy includes provisions for assisting allies within NATO that become victims of a terrorist attack. In short, Oslo has made counterterrorist planning an integral part of Norwegian defense reform.[46]

Although predominantly an Atlantic power, Norway has responded to regional changes in the Baltic littoral. Norway's interest in the Baltic states and the Baltic region emerged largely in the aftermath of the collapse of the Soviet Union. Its roots were partly in the parallel historical experience of the Balts and the Norwegians, with the Balts being occupied by a great power much as Norway was occupied in World War II. In the course of postcommunist transition, Norway took part in Baltic defense reform, focusing its assistance on Latvia. In effect, the four Scandinavian states generated a division-of-labor arrangement, with Denmark focusing on Lithuania, Finland on Estonia, and Sweden on the region as a whole.

KEY TRENDS IN NORDIC DEFENSE POLICY

The evolution of the security policies of the four Scandinavian countries reflects their diverse historical legacies[47] but responds to similar larger trends as well. All four are committed to making their military forces capable of responding to the increasingly global nature of security threats, but because of their individual histories, different institutional arrangements, and differing geostrategic imperatives, they have chosen a variety of approaches. The general trend that all four share is the shift from conscription-based mass mobilization reserves to smaller, more professional forces with higher readiness levels. The second general trend is to shift focus from national territorial defense to multinational operations, emphasizing power-projection capabilities. Depending on the history and geostrategic context of each country, the extent of transformation and relative success differ.

Denmark has arguably made the most progress in reforming its military for power projection international missions. Today the Danish military is almost fully professional at the staffing level and fully committed to NATO power projection. The Danes have shown especially strong support for U.S. military operations, including the one in Iraq in 2003. At the same time, Denmark has all but opted out of the EU military option, in part reacting to the pressure of public opinion in the country. That position may change if the government becomes more adept in charting the course, but it is not likely to be high on Copenhagen's agenda in the foreseeable future.

Sweden's defense reform remains problematic on account of the size of the Swedish armed forces inherited from the Cold War era, the country's massive defense sector, and the long-standing commitment to military nonalignment. Although Sweden has consistently maintained the highest defense budget among the Nordics, large segments of the budget are tied to procurement contracts, giving the defense ministry less room to maneuver than might be evident on paper. The reliance on conscription, with the eleven-month basic training cycle in place and only three to four months of additional training for international deployment, leaves Sweden today with marginal operational forces relative to the overall size of the military. That helps explain why Sweden's international participation is the smallest among all Nordic states. Sweden remains committed to cooperating with NATO but also to staying outside the alliance and working instead within the EU. Stockholm has committed to providing the bulk of an EU combat unit by supplying some twelve hundred Swedish troops to work with two hundred Finns and some Norwegian soldiers, but constraints on the budget and the traditional conscription pattern in the Swedish armed forces may make delivering on the promise problematic for Sweden. The country has clearly begun the process of modifying and dismantling some of its residual defense structures, but it is only beginning the process of building a military for the twenty-first century, especially as regards power-projection capabilities and net-centric warfare.

Norway's defense reform has put it closer to the Danish model, but it still has residual territorial defense capabilities in place. As a NATO member and not an EU member, Oslo is committed to transatlanticism and preserving as much of NATO's viability as possible. Hence its defense reform has shifted decisively toward power projection forces. An exception to that transformation is Norway's frigate program, which enables its navy to provide the maritime protection critical for a country with substantial oil and gas reserves and fisheries that is still vulnerable to Russia's military capabilities.

Finland's defense reform splits the difference, maintaining residual territorial defense while developing new capabilities. Helsinki has been focusing defense expenditures on developing three high-readiness brigades, of which one will be trained for international operations. At the same time, Finland remains fully committed to its traditional territorial defense system because of its immediate proximity to the Russian Federation and continued concern about the direction of Russia's political evolution. Another reason for maintaining a large territorial defense force and ready reserves is Finland's decision not to seek NATO membership. Finland relies on conscription for basic training and selection of the best candidates for further training for specialized units. However, because Finland has not reinvested in the maintenance of its reserves but rather maintained current spending levels, the overall size of the reserves has shrunk over the past decade from approximately 550,000 to some 250,000 men today.

All four Nordic states share the view that the dual NATO/EU enlargement of 2004 reconstituted the Baltic region into an area connecting North and Central Europe with the Baltic littoral. Finland and Denmark are especially sensitive to the new reconfiguration of the region, especially to the role of Germany and Poland following the enlargement of the European Union in 2004.

NOTES

1. WISE-Paris, "Plutonium Proliferation and Non-Proliferation [*sic*]: Sweden—Plutonium Investigation No. 14/15," WISE-Paris, www.wise-paris.org/index.html?/english/ournewsletter/14_15/page3.html&/english/frame/menu.html&/english/frame/band.html.

2. Gunnar Lassinantti, "Small States and Alliances—A Swedish Perspective," in *Small States and Alliances,* ed. Erich Reiter and Heinz Gärtner, 101 (Heidelberg and New York: Physica-Verlag, 2001). The historical portion of this section is based on Lassinantti.

3. Lassinantti, 102.

4. Interviews with Swedish defense and foreign-policy officials, Stockholm, May 2003.

5. Göran Stütz, *Opinion 2003* (Stockholm: Styrelsen för psykologiskt försvar [Psychological Defense Agency], 2003), www.psycdef.se.

6. Mikael Holmström, "Sex av tio säger nej till Nato" [Six out of ten say no to NATO], *Svenska Dagbladet,* January 17, 2004.

7. *Dagens Nyheter,* May 16, 2004.

8. Swedish Defence Commission. *Swedish Security Policy in the Light of International Change* (Stockholm: Swedish Ministry of Defence, 1998), 104.

9. Briefing by Gen. Jan-Gunnar Isberg, Head of Baltic Cooperation Department, Swedish Armed Forces Headquarters, Stockholm, May 27, 2003.

10. Swedish Defence Commission, *Gränsöverskridande sårbarhet—gemensam säkerhet* [Cross-border vulnerability—common security], No. Ds 2001:14 (Stockholm: Försvarsberedningen, 2001), 14, www.regeringen.se/sb/d/108/a/1336.

11. This section is based on Swedish Government Bill 2004/05:5, *Our Future Defense: The Focus of Swedish Defense Policy 2005–2007* (Stockholm: Regeringskansliet, 2004), and briefings in the Swedish Defense Ministry, May 27–28, 2003.

12. Joris Janssen Lok, "Scandinavian Defence Industry: Northern Lights," *Jane's Defence Weekly,* May 4, 2005.

13. Swedish Defence Commission, *Defense for a New Time* (Ds 2004:30), Stockholm: Ministry of Defense, June 1, 2004, www.sweden.gov.se/sb/d/3980/a/24674.

14. "Armed Forces: Sweden," *Janes Sentinel Security Assessment: Central Europe and the Baltics,* February 28, 2005.

15. Swedish Defence Commission, *Säkrare grannskap—osäker värld* Sammanfattning [Summary, *A More Secure Neighbourhood—Insecure World*], No. Ds 2003:8 (Stockholm: Försvarsberedningen, 2003), 3.

16. Kari Möttölä, "Finland, the European Union and NATO—Implications for Security and Defense," in *Small States and Alliances* (see note 2), 114.

17. *Helsingin Sanomat,* February 8, 2004.

18. *Helsingin Sanomat,* June 3, 2004.

19. Author's interviews, Defense Policy Department, Finnish Foreign Ministry, Helsinki, May 19, 2003.

20. Prime Minister's Office, *Finnish Security and Defence Policy 2004,* Government Report 6/2004 (Helsinki: Prime Minister's Office: Publications, 2004), 5.

21. *Finnish Security,* 9.

22. International Institute for Strategic Studies, *The Military Balance 2004–2005,* (London: Routledge, 2004), 87.

23. *Finnish Security,* 111–115.

24. *Finnish Security,* 69.

25. *Finnish Security,* 69.

26. Seppo Nevala, "Speech of the Chief of the Finnish Security Police," *The Finnish Security Police Annual Report 2003, English Summary* (Helsinki: The Finnish Security Police, 2003), www.poliisi.fi/poliisi/supo/home.nsf/pages/446DF80B096 E4FB5C2256BE900418357.

27. This section is based in part on the author's interviews with officials of the Danish Defense Ministry, Copenhagen, May 21–22, 2003.

28. Svend Aage Christensen, "The Danish Experience. Denmark in NATO 1949–1999," in *Small States and Alliances* (see note 2), 95.

29. Interview with Michael Borg-Hansen, Statsministeriet [Prime Minister's Office], Copenhagen, May 21, 2003.

30. Interviews with Danish defense officials, Copenhagen, May 22, 2003. I am also grateful to Per Carlsen, director of the Danish Institute for International Studies (DUPI) for his insights on Danish security policy.

31. Royal Danish Embassy, "Denmark: A Staunch Supporter of the U.S. in Iraq," news release, November 13, 2003, http://64.233.179.104/search?q=cache:MUVB JwUaGoEJ:www.denmarkemb.org/news/.

32. United States Mission to NATO, "Denmark," Allied Contributions to the War against Terrorism, nato.usmission.gov/Contributions/Denmark.htm.

33. "Unpopularity Begins at Home: Denmark," *The Economist*," March 20, 2004, 52.

34. British Broadcasting Corporation, "Danish Centre-Right Win New Term," *BBC News*, February 8, 2005, http://news.bbc.co.uk/1/hi/world/europe/4245239 .stm.

35. Danish Defence, Defence Command Denmark, "The Danish Defence Agreement 2005–2009," news release, June 7, 2004, http://forsvaret.dk/FKO/eng/ Defence+Agreement/default.htm?Mode=Print&Site=fko.

36. "Danish Defence Agreement 2005–2009."

37. "Armed Forces: Denmark," *Jane's Sentinel Security Assessment—Western Europe*, August 3, 2005.

38. "Danish Defence Agreement 2005–2009."

39. "Danish Defence Agreement 2005–2009."

40. Norwegian Ministry of Defence, *The Long-Term Defence Plan for 2002–2005* (Oslo: Ministry of Defense), www.odin.dep.no/fd/engelsk/publ/veiledninger/ 010011-120018/dok-bn.html.

41. Norwegian Ministry of Defence, *The Long-Term Defence Plan for 2002–2005.*

42. Briefing by Norwegian defense officials, Norwegian Defense Ministry, Oslo, May 30, 2003.

43. Norwegian Defense Department, *The Further Modernisation of the Norwegian Armed Forces 2005–2008*, Proposition to Parliament No. 42 (2003–2004), Short Version (Oslo: Norwegian Defense Department, 2004).

44. "Armed Forces: Norway," *Jane's Sentinel and Security Assessment-Western Europe*, February 24, 2005.

45. Norwegian Defense Department, *The Further Modernisation of the Norwegian Armed Forces 2005–2008*, Proposition to Parliament No. 42 (2003–2004), Short Version (Oslo: Norwegian Defense Department, 2004).

46. Norwegian Ministry of Defence. *Norway's Future Defense, The Implementation Proposition: A Short Version of Government Proposition No. 55, 2001–2002* (Oslo: Norwegian Ministry of Defence, 2002).

47. Interview with Tom Ries, Helsinki, May 23, 2003. I am grateful to Tomas Ries for providing his insights for this comparative net assessment of Nordic defense policies.

The Northeastern Littoral:
Russia and the Baltic States

FROM THE DOMINANT TO AN "OUTSIDE" BALTIC POWER

The collapse of the USSR has had a profound impact on Russia's position in the Baltic littoral, reversing three centuries of expansion and ending the country's status as a preeminent Baltic power. For Russia, the geostrategic transformation was even more profound on account of the scope of its systemic implosion, the continued weakness of Russian state institutions, and the centrifugal ethnic forces within the Russian Federation. After the collapse of the Soviet Union Russia emerged with roughly half of the USSR's population, three quarters of its territory. And—though it retained the majority of its residual military power, including nuclear weapons—the quality of Russia's military force deteriorated rapidly.[1] At the same time as it has struggled to build a working nation-state, Russia has had to face the consequences of the reversal of three hundred years of colonization and imperial expansion, compounded by turmoil in the wake of the country's early transition to a market economy. The end of the Cold War seems to have invalidated the Russian dictum that "empire is fate," and nowhere more than in the Baltic littoral.

The fragmentation of the USSR into fifteen independent states was unlike any experience in Russia's history. It negated the principles of imperial state building that had defined the Russian state in the past. Independent Ukraine in the western near abroad and independent Estonia, Latvia, and Lithuania in the Baltic region have become the critical blocks to any future Russian imperial drive into North and Central Europe. The 1991 breakup of the Warsaw Pact and Russia's loss of control over eastern Central Europe would not have been sufficient in and of themselves to foreclose the imperial option, but the sovereignty of Ukraine and the Baltic states has forced Russia to contemplate a national future without empire. The dual enlargement of

NATO and the EU in 2004 into the Baltic littoral has symbolized the dramatic decline of direct Russian influence in the region. Inasmuch as the future of Russia's influence in Ukraine is still a matter of contention—albeit in the aftermath of the 2004 Ukrainian "Orange Revolution" it is no longer a given that Moscow could easily bring Kiev back into the fold—in the Baltic littoral Russia's options are circumscribed by the presence of Euro-Atlantic structures.

The decline of Russia's power position in the Baltic region stems from the confluence of three problems central to Russian security: the persistent economic weakness of the Kaliningrad District, the continuing decline of its military, and continuing tension in relations with the Baltic states over the legacy of the Cold War and the status of Russian ethnic diaspora.[2] The last named has been an especially difficult problem. While the military and economic problems are being addressed in the EU-wide context, the historical and ethnic burden has a direct impact on Russia's bilateral relations with the Baltic states. For the Balts the memory of widespread deportations that lasted through 1949, combined with in-migration of Russians, Ukrainians, and Belorussians during Soviet occupation has made it difficult for them to consider Russia anything but a residual threat to their security. The Balts consider Soviet Russia's colonization to have been a state policy aimed at diluting their national identity and undermining their claim to self-determination. The Soviet policy proved especially damaging in Latvia, where on the eve of independence only 52 percent of Latvia's population remained ethnically Latvian, but all three Baltic states have emerged from communism with lower percentages of their national populations than before World War II.

Resentment over Soviet colonization during the Cold War is compounded by the searing memory of the 1939 Ribbentrop-Molotov pact and the Soviet aggression that followed. In that historical context the Baltics do not consider themselves to be "successor states" to the Soviet Union; rather, they see themselves as sovereign states that fell victim to Russian imperialism. In 2005 the governments of the Baltic states were divided over the issue of whether to send delegations to Moscow to celebrate the 60th anniversary of the end of World War II. The insistence on their sovereignty is a constitutive element of Baltic identity, with Russia perceived as the historic adversary.

As a declining power in the Nordic-Baltic area, Russia has sought since 1991 to limit further damage to its position by asserting its rights in Kaliningrad and remaining engaged in the region while resisting NATO enlargement to its borders. Hence Russian security policy in the Baltic has been channeled in two directions: (1) sustaining Kaliningrad while attempting to stabilize relations with Estonia, Latvia, and Lithuania to retain a modicum of its former influence; and (2) seeking to prevent the enlargement of NATO into the Baltic littoral or, failing that, limiting the effectiveness of NATO. In contrast to its staunch opposition to NATO enlargement, Moscow's views on EU enlargement into the Baltic have been more ambivalent. On the one hand, Russia has looked at EU enlargement into the region as yet another act of continued Western encroachment into its historical sphere of influence; on the other hand, it has recognized the economic opportunity that EU proximity has presented to Russia.

Russia's status as an "outside power" is highlighted by the continued potential threat posed to the Baltics by its residual military power, mainly the Baltic Fleet and its bases in the Kaliningrad District. Historically, the Baltic coastal area, with its warm-water ports, has been at the heart of Russian regional security and imperial ambitions. That is never forgotten by the Baltic states, nor by Finland and Poland. In the past, a dominant position in the Baltic validated Russia's claim to be a great European power, and it was the precondition for projecting Russian naval power in the north. The significance of the Baltic to Russian security grew exponentially in the Soviet period, especially in the last two decades of communist power when, as of the late 1970s, Moscow built a modern, oceangoing navy that enabled it to contest the American domination of the Atlantic.

Today in Moscow's view the Baltic Sea region remains vital to Russian security, and therefore it is an area where Russia is committed to contesting for influence. Thus even though Russian military capabilities have declined, the imperial legacy of mutual suspicion between Russia and the Baltic states remains a central issue in the region's security. The history of Russian imperialism has given particular salience to the quest for NATO membership for the Baltic states, which until virtually the last moment Moscow declared to be an intrusion into the area it has historically claimed as its "window to the West." Conversely, for the Baltic states, NATO membership has carried with it first and foremost the traditional security guarantee in line with the "old NATO" of the Cold War era. For both Russia and the Baltic states, the key barometer of regional security is the status of the Kaliningrad District—an enclave of the Russian Federation surrounded by the territory of Lithuania and Poland and, since the "dual enlargement" of 2004, an area inside the enlarged European Union and NATO.

KALININGRAD IN REGIONAL SECURITY: THE ECONOMIC DIMENSION

Russia's continued assertion of full sovereignty over the Kaliningrad District and the remaining Russian military installations in the enclave have defined its place in Baltic security. However, although residual military issues and visa transit issues have been given the most prominence in Western analyses, the economic conditions in the enclave are likely to determine Kaliningrad's future

place in the region. Since 1991, Kaliningrad has been an economically de-
pressed region, with declining industrial and agricultural output and declining
oil production. It has also been a growing burden on Russia's treasury. The key
question about Kaliningrad is whether it can overcome the economic crisis and
become an economically stable outpost of Russia or will continue to flounder
and foster regional instability.

Kaliningrad is a quintessentially peripheral enclave, tucked away in the
corner of the eastern Baltic. Geographically detached from the Russian Federation and insulated from it by Lithuania and Poland, Kaliningrad must rely on
regional trade links to complement its trade with Russia in order to sustain its
economy, as direct subsidies from the Russian government are not enough. The
economic impact of the district's insularity was somewhat less pressing in the
years before EU enlargement; Kaliningrad had developed vigorous cross-border
trade with Poland and Lithuania. Still, even before the introduction of the EU-
mandated visa requirement, economic conditions in Kaliningrad were stark.
While at the beginning of the 1990s Kaliningrad's economy rested on a combination of fishing, machine building, and wood processing, by the end of the
decade the largest source of revenue came from services and trade, especially
small-scale cross-border trade. By 1998, agricultural output of the enclave fell
to 45 percent of the 1990 level, while its oil production, which has been its principal export, fell to 50 percent of the 1990 level. Smuggling has remained an
important part of Kaliningrad's economy, compounding the problem of rising
crime. More important, in the 1990s Kaliningrad continued to slide into debt.
In 2001 its indebtedness stood at 1.3 billion rubles, with the estimate that ser-
vicing the debt would consume 58 percent of the region's budget.[3]

Kaliningrad also suffered severe economic disruptions following the 1998
Russian crisis, with its output dropping by 62 percent compared to 1990.[4] Even
so, thanks to the creation of the Special Economic Zone (SEZ), which eased investment and trade rules, Kaliningrad was able to weather the worst. The SEZ
in Kaliningrad, introduced in 1991 and modified by the 1996 Law on the Kaliningrad SEZ, confirmed the status of Kaliningrad as part of the Russian state and
gave it a duty-free status on goods imports into Kaliningrad, as well as exemp-
tion from duties on goods manufactured in Kaliningrad and exported to Russia.
Since 1998 Kaliningrad has been subjected to an import quota on 35 categories
of goods, which are then auctioned off. Goods above the quota limits enter Russian customs territory and are subject to regular customs procedures. Overall, the
SEZ helped the enclave survive the crisis, but with fewer than a million residents, Kaliningrad has inherent limitations on its growth potential.

The future of economic development in Kaliningrad, especially its "free
economic zone" status, irrespective of various plans and government decisions, will ultimately depend on one country within the European Union that

has the means to make a difference in the region: Germany. The future of German-Russian relations is critical to Kaliningrad's economic prospects, with obvious implications for the region's economy as a whole. If, in light of the 2004 EU enlargement up to the borders of Kaliningrad, the enclave can hope for substantial direct foreign investment, it will have to come principally from Germany. Total foreign investment in Kaliningrad District in 2003 was more than $56.2 million, of which direct foreign investment was slightly less than $14 million, or less than 24 percent of the total. That is indicative of the potential for economic transformation in the enclave if German-Russian relations continue to progress. Though low overall, foreign investment in Kaliningrad increased between 2000 and 2003 by more than 200 percent.[5]

The 2004 EU enlargement has offered an opportunity for an economic turnaround in Kaliningrad. The district, though small in terms of geography and population, has since become a focal point in the discussions between the European Union and the Russian Federation, including talks about further development of the EU's regional cooperative initiatives. The most obvious consequence of the 2004 dual enlargement is that Kaliningrad is no longer just the border area between Russia and NATO but has in fact become an internal EU enclave. Kaliningrad's economy is suspended between Russia and the European Union. Trade flows before 2004 are indicative of the region's current position: On average, 40 percent of Kaliningrad's trade was with the Russian mainland, 20–25 percent with the old 15 EU states, and 20 percent with the new ones, essentially Poland and Lithuania.[6] While Russia remained the principal economic partner of Kaliningrad, it was followed by Poland, which in 2000 accounted for 32.4 percent and in 2001 for 27.5 percent of Kaliningrad's exports. Germany accounted for 22–25 percent of Kaliningrad's import trade over the past several years, followed by Poland and Lithuania.[7]

After 2004, the European Union was the obvious regional trading partner for Kaliningrad. Today approximately 40 percent of Kaliningrad's trade is with the EU original 15, 30 percent is with Poland and Lithuania, and another 5–7 percent with the rest of the newly acceded EU states. Hence after the 2004 enlargement, the European Union accounts for 75 percent of Kaliningrad's foreign trade.[8] In short, Kaliningrad takes on an intermediary position between Europe and Russia in trade. Because of its direct exposure to the West and its value to Russia as an intermediary, Kaliningrad has been more responsive to the pressures of economic change than the rest of the Russian Federations, both in negative and positive terms, experiencing deeper recessions during the times of economic downturn and faster economic growth during times of economic expansion.[9] In the coming years, especially if Russia becomes a member of the WTO, Kaliningrad has the potential to become a laboratory for the new economic partnership between the European Union and Russia, with important consequences for the regional security equation. If that fails, it will continue to be a source of instability and a drain on the Russian treasury.

Among the new EU countries in the region, Kaliningrad has had special economic relations with Poland and Lithuania. Poland has become an important economic partner in part because of the country's dynamic economic growth in the mid-1990s, though as early as May 1992 Presidents Lech Walesa and Boris Yeltsin had signed an agreement on cooperation between Kaliningrad and the northeastern regions of Poland.[10] More important, until Poland joined the EU and was obligated by the Schengen provisions to increase border controls, Kaliningrad had a visa-free travel agreement with Poland in keeping with Polish-Russian border agreements. That has generated the largest cross-border trade for Kaliningrad. Poland was also the first country to open a consulate in Kaliningrad, with a reciprocal consul assigned to the Russian consulate in Gdansk. Moreover, though Poland supported the idea of a Free Economic Zone in Kaliningrad, it was not interested in internationalizing it, preferring bilateral arrangements. Because of its historically bad relations with Russia, Poland most of all wanted to demilitarize the district as much as possible and was opposed to an earlier scheme, briefly discussed by Germany and Russia, to resettle a large number of Volga Germans in Kaliningrad.

As has been the case with Poland, Lithuania's economic ties have always been set against the larger historical context. Lithuania has been the most proactive in the region in making claims on Kaliningrad, exceeding those of the Poles, who principally focused their efforts on reducing the military potential of Russia. In the early 1990s, there was a clear sentiment among a sizable segment of the Lithuanian population that the region's territory should actually belong to the Lithuanian state. That position was represented by both nationalists and the Lithuanian exile community in the West, especially in the United States, which claimed that either parts of "Lithuania Minor" or the entire Kaliningrad region should be restored to the Lithuanian state.[11] For Lithuania, Russian military presence in Kaliningrad has remained the central concern and preoccupation, dominating all the economic considerations and driving the country's security policy and its overall objective of joining NATO at the earliest possible opportunity.

KALININGRAD AND RUSSIA'S RESIDUAL MILITARY CAPABILITIES IN THE BALTIC

The demise of the Soviet Union has had a lasting impact on Russia's military posture and on the Baltic Fleet's deployment in Kaliningrad, yet it is in the

Baltic region more than in other parts of the Russian Federation that the precipitous decline of Russian military power has been partly arrested. Notwithstanding its decline in the 1990s, today the Baltic Fleet is arguably the best organized and run component of the Russian armed forces. That is in part a legacy of effective management by its commander between 1991 and 2000, and the subsequent governor of the Kaliningrad District, Adm. Vladimir Yegorov. The importance of the Baltic dimension to Russian security strategy is reflected in the institutional arrangements for the Baltic command. The commander of the Baltic Fleet, who also commanded the Kaliningrad Special Defense District (KOOR) until its dissolution in 1997, reports directly to the chief of staff of the Russian armed forces and to the minister of defense. The command center for the Baltic Fleet is located in Kaliningrad.

The Baltic Fleet has been relatively well maintained, albeit reduced in size. Russian ground forces in the Kaliningrad District were reduced by 40 percent over the course of the 1990s, today numbering approximately twenty-five thousand.[12] The Baltic Fleet equipment is relatively new, with roughly 70 percent of the equipment being less than fifteen years old. Likewise, the aircraft and helicopters allocated to the enclave are in good condition compared to Russian deployments elsewhere. More significant, however, for the overall security equation along the Baltic littoral, is that Russian naval forces in the Baltic are now configured for defensive missions, and Russia has long abandoned the Cold War–era strategy of preparing a strike at the Danish Straits. Any return to a similar offensive strategy would require the reintroduction of heavy naval ships, decommissioned in the 1990s, and it would take several years to prepare.

There is a political dimension to continued viability of the Baltic Fleet that the Russians have articulated quite unequivocally on several occasions. The Fleet was at times described as an implicit deterrent to NATO and EU enlargement into the Baltic region. In September 2002 Speaker of the Federation Council Sergey Mironov claimed that the existence of the Baltic Fleet was a "weighty argument in talks with Europe over EU and NATO expansion."[13] Speaking at the Baltic Fleet's main naval base in Baltiysk, Mironov asserted that the Baltic Fleet was crucial to defending Russia's strategic interests in the Baltic and hence enhancing its capabilities and readiness was a priority. Although the alleged capability of the Baltic Fleet ultimately proved insufficient to prevent NATO and EU enlargement, that and similar assertions by Russian politicians suggest the continuing importance of Baltic military capabilities for Russia's overall position in the region. Following the dual EU/NATO enlargement, Moscow considers the Baltic Fleet the foundation for any future offensive strategy.

Senior Russian military officials have explicitly expressed the view that they continue to look at NATO as an adversary. In the summer of 2004, Adm. Vladimir Valuyev, the new commander of the Baltic Fleet, warned on Russian

NTV television that as long as NATO behaved peacefully, the Baltic Fleet would confine itself to peaceful tasks, but "if the situation is escalated, we'll always be ready to take appropriate action."[14] The Russians have frequently commented on the close surveillance that the Baltic Fleet is subject to whenever it operates in the Baltic Sea—procedures that Russian commanders interpret as the sign of continued fear on NATO's part of the Baltic Fleet's capabilities and as an indicator of NATO's offensive intentions.

It is unlikely that Moscow will downgrade the significance of the Kaliningrad military enclave anytime soon, especially since the dual enlargement has increased the sense of Kaliningrad's isolation and the overall division between the enlarged EU/NATO and the Russian Federation. In the coming years, the Baltic Fleet is likely to gain in importance as the primary vehicle for Russia's power projection in the Baltic. The Kaliningrad Special Defense Area (KOOR) was established in 1994 and operated until 1997. The Baltic Fleet headquarters and main base were in the KOOR (in Kaliningrad and Baltiysk, respectively), and its second base was in Kronshtadt near St. Petersburg. In effect, the KOOR was linked to the larger defense structure of the Russian Federation's armed forces. Though reduced in size, the Russian forces in the KOOR were still large enough to pose a potential offensive threat, especially compared to the forces deployed by Russia's neighbors in the immediate vicinity of the region. The upgraded status of the Baltic Fleet was made clear when, after the KOOR was abolished in 1997, the remainder of its ground forces, including the Eleventh Independent Army, were subordinated to the commander of the Baltic Fleet. In mid-1996, on the eve of KOOR dissolution, the garrison was estimated at twenty-four thousand ground troops of the Eleventh Guards Combined Arms Army, including one tank division and three motorized rifle divisions, three artillery brigades, surface-to-surface and surface-to-air missiles, and attack helicopters. These forces, although reduced, constitute the residual military component of the Baltic Fleet's ground deployment.

Today the naval component of the Baltic Fleet consists of three cruisers, two destroyers, eighteen frigates, sixty-five patrol boats, and 195 combat aircraft, together with one brigade of naval infantry and two regiments of coastal defense artillery. The official Russian figure on total military personnel in Kaliningrad is approximately one hundred thousand; however, the real figure is estimated at closer to two hundred thousand overall.[15] Moscow's continued investment in the Kaliningrad forces is central to the argument, put forward forcefully by Russian nationalists, that the Kaliningrad military bases must be maintained and strengthened, especially after the 2004 dual enlargement, because they constitute the only outpost of Russia in the northeast.

The Baltic Fleet was reformed between 1997 and 1998 and today constitutes an overall smaller force than during the Cold War and its immediate aftermath. Nevertheless, it remains viable. The majority of the naval vessels deployed in Kaliningrad and the aircraft and helicopters currently in service in the region are modern and expected to remain in service through 2010. The capabilities today are mainly defensive, with the greatest emphasis being placed on antisubmarine and demining operations. The scope of the Baltic Fleet's naval exercises suggests that its principal goal in the event of conflict would be to paralyze naval traffic in the Baltic. Land forces under the command of the Baltic Fleet are considered less ready than the naval component and, based on military exercises called Zapad-99, their task in the event of conflict would be to provide territorial defense and to link up with land forces in Belarus. Although land personnel have been reduced from Cold War levels, they maintain high readiness levels and train inside as well as outside the Kaliningrad enclave; for example, in 1999–2000 several mechanized and naval infantry units from Kaliningrad were deployed in the Chechen campaign.[16]

Russian military presence remains the *sine qua non* of Moscow's policy toward the region.[17] Territorial defense is increasingly viewed as a central strategy for the enclave. At the center of the debate on Kaliningrad's military future is whether in fact the island-mainland metaphor should apply to the relationship between the District and the Russian state.[18] The military deployment will depend on whether Kaliningrad is considered a Russian island in the Baltic Sea or an isolated enclave separated from the mainland. As some have argued, moving from the continental to maritime metaphor would set aside the most contentious issues, such as the question of transit through Lithuania and Poland and large-scale ground-force deployments. The decision is Russia's to make, but opting for a ferry link over the current territorial access from Belarus would change the entire security dynamic of the district, and it would permit military reconfiguration of the enclave.

Kaliningrad has another added value for the Russian military. Because of Russia's withdrawal from Germany and Poland, Kaliningrad is now the best intelligence-collecting station the Russians have in the region for radar and radio transmission, and the continued gathering of intelligence is the most valuable function of the residual Russian military deployment there. Even though the Baltic littoral was strategically reconfigured after the disintegration of the Warsaw Pact, the Baltiysk base continues to be the Russians' premier data-gathering station. Kaliningrad military deployments contribute to the territorial defense of the Russian Federation as a whole, as they provide for the defense of the links connecting the enclave to the mainland. They are integrated with the Federation's early-warning system. Last but not least, the enclave gives Russia rare residual leverage for area control in the central Baltic Sea and in the Gulf of Finland.

The final, and potentially most explosive, residual military issue concerning the Kaliningrad enclave is the ongoing concern in the NATO alliance that Russia may be continuing to station tactical nuclear weapons there. Such reports, based on American intelligence, were leaked to the press in January 2001. They were rejected by both the Russian foreign ministry and the Command of the Baltic Fleet, but concerns about tactical nuclear weapons in Kaliningrad remain. Moreover, should Russia choose to deploy tactical nuclear weapons in the enclave, there is no binding treaty agreement that would prevent it from doing so other than the declaratory policy of making the Baltic Sea region a nonnuclear zone. In fact, it is possible that the Soviet Union had deployed tactical nuclear warheads in Kaliningrad beginning in the 1960s and that the Russian Federation simply never pulled the weapons out. While any future Russian decision to deploy nuclear weapons in Kaliningrad would be politically explosive, there are no technical problems per se that would prevent Moscow from following through on such a decision.

RUSSIAN RELATIONS WITH NATO AND THE EU: A REGIONAL DIMENSION

The decline of Russia's position in the Baltic in the course of the 1990s was symbolized by the pullout of Russian troops from the Baltic states between 1993 and 1994, tensions over the voting rights and citizenship requirements for the non-Baltic ethnics, and strained economic relations between Russia and the Baltic states, which often charged that Russia engaged in outright economic blockade to bring them to heel. The biggest change in Russia's position vis-à-vis the Baltics was its grudging recognition of the fact that Estonia, Latvia, and Lithuania could not be folded into Russia's near abroad in the same fashion as other CIS states.[19] Russia's opposition to NATO enlargement into the Baltic region was the strongest between 1994 and 1997, with the expectation that while enlargement into Central Europe would establish the new boundaries of Western presence in the region, those boundaries could not be allowed to move farther. The Russian government repeatedly denounced the idea of NATO enlargement into the region as a direct challenge to its security position and as a threat to European stability.

Following the November 2002 Prague declaration that the upcoming round of NATO enlargement would include Estonia, Latvia, and Lithuania, Russia began to come to terms with the idea that had seemed an anathema when the Soviet empire began to unravel: that NATO would reach Russia's borders by entering the area of the former USSR itself. During the Prague summit, Russian Foreign Minister Sergey Ivanov tried to play down the issue, while President George W. Bush made an effort during his visit to St. Petersburg immediately after the Prague NATO summit to reassure Russia's President Vladimir Putin that NATO enlargement would in no way damage Russia's security. Still, it was impossible to avoid the overall thrust of the new security environment in the Baltic region.

Russia's grudging acceptance of NATO enlargement into the Baltic littoral was dictated in part by a closer Russian-American relationship in the aftermath of the September 11 terrorist attack against the World Trade Center and the Pentagon. However, Russia's negative view of NATO enlargement into the Baltic area continued into 2005, though the dual enlargement should have made it quite obvious to Moscow that Russia's objections have not had the desired effect on the Western powers. Speaking at a press conference in Brussels following a meeting of the Russia-NATO Council on April 2, 2004, Russia's Foreign Minister Sergey Lavrov repeated that Russia would never favor NATO enlargement, that Russia's attitude toward the expansion into the Baltic remained "negative," and that enlargement was a "mistake."[20] At the same time, however, Lavrov recognized that Russia's ability to influence NATO's decision making was limited, while Washington clearly rejected the idea that Moscow was in a position to redline the northern area of its near abroad.

Russia looks at NATO's move into the Baltic area principally as enlargement into the territory of the former USSR, where Russia has tried to maintain its special position. Moscow is convinced that the next step for NATO might be enlargement into Ukraine, Moldova, Georgia, Uzbekistan, and other central Asian countries, especially as the American war against Islamic terrorism continues to focus on the southern periphery of the former Soviet Union. In that sense, failure to prevent enlargement of NATO into the Baltic littoral has had a larger dimension for Russia's foreign and security policy, as it marked the crossing of a critical psychological barrier. Continued NATO enlargement, especially if it were to include central Asia, is likely to be interpreted in Moscow as another step toward the encirclement of Russia.

A signal of the continued tension between Russia and NATO over enlargement was Moscow's reaction to NATO's decision to deploy aircraft to defend the airspace of the new Baltic members of the alliance. Increasingly, especially as Russian-American relations began to deteriorate in early 2005, Moscow asserted that it might be compelled to rethink its strategy if what it called an "aggressive NATO strategy" continued unchanged. But Russia clearly recognized the limitations of its position. In February 2005 Moscow sent a signal that it was still interested in exploring closer cooperation with NATO, when Russia Defense Minister Sergey Ivanov indicated that Russia was preparing a peacekeeping force that could work with NATO. Russia also sent ships to the eastern Mediterranean to assist NATO in monitoring shipping for WMD and terrorist activities.[21] Clearly, Russia's opposition to NATO enlargement was mixed with a dose of political realism.

Paradoxically, although Russia resisted NATO enlargement to a greater degree than EU enlargement, the latter may prove more problematic for Russia's security in the long run. If the past is any indication, the immediate impact of Central European and Baltic membership in the EU may cost Russia significantly in economic terms. For example, after Austria, Finland, and Sweden joined the EU, estimated Russian economic losses in trade ran about $100 million annually.[22] In the wake of the 2004 EU enlargement, the economic gap between Russia and the new EU members in the region is likely to deepen rapidly. Even though trade between Kaliningrad and the EU initially increased, Schengen regulations will significantly limit the movement of Russians into the region and raise serious questions about the long-term economic viability of Kaliningrad. If Russia remains committed to sustaining Kaliningrad, the projected decline in exports from there will require an increase in subsidies to the enclave from the Federation's budget. The 2004 EU enlargement is also likely to increase Russia's sense of isolation; regional cooperation that prior to enlargement focused on Russia may in future focus within the Baltic Schengen boundary. The most important long-term factor is that, in contrast to Ukraine, which in 2005 made overtures to begin the process of EU accession, the Russian Federation is unlikely to apply for even associate EU membership in the foreseeable future.

Visa-free access to Kaliningrad after EU enlargement was a critical issue in Moscow's relations with Brussels, as well as a bone of contention in its bilateral relations with Lithuania and Poland. Originally Russia demanded transit corridors through Poland and Lithuania as the optimal solution to the access issue, but both Poland and Lithuania rejected the demand on the grounds that the route's extraterritoriality would have been incompatible with their laws and EU regulations. Russian access to Kaliningrad through Lithuania proved the most important issue in negotiations, and the EU went through several iterations of possible arrangements for border transit with Russia before both sides accepted an arrangement that facilitated transit and did not violate EU laws.

On April 18, 2003, in the run-up to EU enlargement, a solution was agreed to when Russia, Lithuania, and the EU clinched a deal on transit access to Kaliningrad. Under the arrangement Russian citizens would be allowed to pass through Lithuania using the so-called Facilitated Transit Documents (FRD) and the Facilitated Railway Transit Documents (FRTD), issued free of charge and with minimal paperwork. The program's financing was settled on February 28, 2003, when the EU and Lithuania signed a financing memorandum that provided Vilnius with €12 million in financial support to cover the costs of the new arrangement. In effect, the EU financed 100 percent of the project—a clear signal of how important and sensitive the transit issue has been in EU-Russian relations. The agreement went into effect July 1, 2003, and ended the previous period of visa-free travel for Russians through Lithuania.[23]

Poland introduced visas for Russian citizens on October 1, 2003, in anticipation of the country's EU accession. At first, Warsaw offered Moscow a nonreciprocal arrangement of the kind it established with Ukraine, whereby the Poles would have been able to travel to Russia visa-free and Russians would receive their visas to Poland free of charge. The Russian side rejected the offer as not equitable and, following further negotiations, Poland and Russia established a new reciprocal visa agreement but with nonreciprocal exception for Kaliningrad. The arrangement allows the residents of Kaliningrad to obtain Polish visas free of charge, while other citizens of the Russian Federation must pay for their visas to Poland. Poles traveling to Kaliningrad also obtain their visas to the enclave free of charge. However, Russians are not required to have transit visas to cross Poland if they are traveling to Germany or beyond, as long as they have valid Schengen visas.[24]

Since EU enlargement Russians have been required to have a valid passport and visas for transit, but Poland, Lithuania, and Sweden have increased the number of consular facilities to reduce the wait time. Other provisions of the agreement include the issuance of multiple-entry visas for transit to and from Kaliningrad.

The introduction of visa requirements by Poland and Lithuania prior to their entry into the EU in 2004 had the effect of increasing Kaliningrad's isolation from mainland Russia. Following the establishment of the new visa regime, Russian President Vladimir Putin made a symbolic gesture to reaffirm Russia's sovereignty over the enclave when he announced the opening of a new low-cost travel link between Moscow and Kaliningrad to counter the effects of the new visa arrangements.[25]

Notwithstanding friction over the Kaliningrad transit access in the wake of the 2004 EU enlargement, the EU remains Russia's largest trading partner, with over half of all Russia's exports going to the enlarged EU. Russia has become the EU's fourth largest export market, after the United States, Switzerland, and Japan. In 2003 Russia's exports to the EU amounted to €51.5 billion, the majority of it in energy products. The same year Russia was the EU's fifth largest trading partner, importing €33 billion in European goods. Russia has benefited from direct EU technical assistance (Tacis), a European initiative for Eastern Europe, Caucasus, and Central Asia (subsequently succeeded by the EU-Russia Cooperation Program). The initiative was extended to the Kaliningrad enclave in 1991; since then it has benefited the Russian Federation as a whole, providing close to €2.5 billion in assistance for more than 1,500 projects in the Russian Federation.[26] Roughly €40 million has been earmarked for direct EU aid to the Kaliningrad enclave, and a Tacis (EU-Russia Cooperation Program) office is in place in the city of Kaliningrad.[27]

RUSSIA'S CHOICE: THE FUTURE STATUS OF KALININGRAD

Geography is at the heart of the two intersecting currents that will define Russia's security position in the Baltic region: Russia's relationship to Kaliningrad as its severed peripheral outpost and the relationship of Kaliningrad to the Nordic/Central European EU/NATO member states that will continue to eye with suspicion Russia's intentions in the region. Kaliningrad's geostrategic dilemma is that the Second World War/Cold War legacy still remains central to its security. To its neighbors, Kaliningrad is the bellwether of Russia's security policy in the region. Kaliningrad also constitutes a larger EU problem: Its overlapping security, economic, environmental, and political impact cannot be separated from the overall relationship between Russia and the West. Russia's military bases, trade, transit, and visa issues all point to the overarching question of Russia's power position in the Baltic. In all of those dimensions, Kaliningrad is the nexus of the problem and a symbol of Russia's decline in the region.

By 2005, the initial debates on the future of Kaliningrad, first cast in a simplistic dichotomous fashion—with Kaliningrad becoming either a "second Cuba" menacing its neighbors or a "Baltic Hong Kong" free-trade haven contributing to shared prosperity and peace—were eclipsed by the more complex, if less satisfying, reality on the ground. The facile parallels, drawn early on between Kaliningrad's geostrategic position and that of East Prussia of the interwar period, have been jettisoned. Still, even though prospects of a territorial dispute like the one that had fractured German-Polish relations over the "corridor" issue before World War II are a remote academic exercise, Kaliningrad remains a problem for Russia's position in the region and in its relations with Europe. Every time the relationship cools, the issue of the enclave's potential rearmament comes to the fore.

The question of the status of Kaliningrad also brings with it the risk of revisiting the legacy of German-Russian relations after World War II. Although the issue is not currently on the agenda, the status of Kaliningrad holds the potential of bringing up the question of compensation to the German expellees from the region. The same problem concerning the compensation of German expellees from the western territories of Poland transferred to it after the war has already become a disruptive issue in German-Polish relations. It is possible that a similar issue may arise in German-Russian relations over expellees from former East Prussia. At the close of World War II, German inhabitants of Königsberg and its environs who had survived the especially bitter fighting and the harsh Russian occupation were expelled and replaced with in-migrants from Russia, Belarussia, and Ukraine. The region was quickly Russified and Sovietized; about two-thirds of today's population were born in the region.[28] But the historical memory of German presence along the Baltic rim is likely to persist as long as the German and Russian survivors of the war are alive.

During the Soviet era, Kaliningrad was one of the most heavily militarized regions of the USSR, with limited access even for Soviet citizens. The shadow of that past still looms over the region. In essence, Soviet Kaliningrad was both a major naval base and a strategic reserves base for the Soviet armed forces preparing for an attack against NATO. In 1956 the headquarters for the Soviet Baltic Fleet were moved from Leningrad to Kaliningrad, with Baltiysk becoming a major naval base in the region. The district also became host to major Soviet ground, air, and air-defense deployments. That changed drastically with the collapse of the USSR and the independence of the Baltic states, which meant a loss of the majority of Russian naval bases in the region—and conversely, raised the overall importance of Baltiysk and Kaliningrad to Russian military posture in the Baltic. In effect, along with St. Petersburg, Kaliningrad became the only additional Russian naval base on the Baltic Sea deep in the Gulf of Finland. The Baltic states, Poland, and Finland regard the enclave as the continuation of that former deployment.

Today, more important than its role as the base for Baltic naval operation is Kaliningrad's role as a forward base for air and air defense forces. As Russia's enthusiasm for democratization and partnership with the United States began to cool in the mid-1990s, Kaliningrad increasingly became an area of considerable preoccupation for the Russian military planners. Although originally the Russians planned to reduce the size of the military in the region to 25,000, those reductions were limited in 1994 to the 40,000–45,000 target size of the armed forces. In the course of NATO enlargement negotiations, Moscow both implicitly and explicitly threatened to increase the size of the military deployment in the Kaliningrad District. To this day, the leverage that Russia has had in manipulating the size of the Kaliningrad deployment stems from the fact that the size of Russia's forces in the district will always numerically overshadow the size of the forces that the newly independent Baltic states can put in place, regardless of the speed with which they are trying to modernize their military forces. The continued high level of militarization of the Kaliningrad District has been the central concern of the Baltic states. For them as well as for Poland, Russia's continued military deployment in Kaliningrad has been a source of worry—and of their desire for NATO membership.

Transit rights for Russia through Lithuania and Poland have remained a bone of contention often laden with heavy symbolism on both sides. Lithuania finds itself in the most exposed position on the issue of Russian transit, as the main rail links to Kaliningrad run through it, including its largest cities. Though transit through Lithuania is highly symbolic in the context of the two countries' bilateral relations and in terms of the overall security situation in the region, its military importance to Russia should not be overstated. Only a fraction of Russia's military transport takes place via the rail link in Lithuania, the majority moving by sea. The most symbolic issue in the mid-1990s for both Poland and Lithuania was the Russian proposal to build a "corridor" highway and an upgraded link that would give Russia and Belarus better access to the Baltic ports, although in the 1990s Poland and Lithuania approved the request to upgrade their rail and road network to facilitate better communications between Belarus and Kaliningrad. Today the Lithuanians and the Poles question whether the transit issue has ever been an end in itself or a means of asserting Russia's continued prerogative in the area.

The key dilemma for the Baltic region is that because Kaliningrad is a part of Russia, its defense is the responsibility of the Russian Federation, and hence Russia remains physically planted in the region. It is highly unlikely that Kaliningrad will be demilitarized, as has been suggested at times, because that would force Russia to yield its principal military outpost in the region. However, the greatest challenge of Kaliningrad's regional position is not the one posed to the Baltic states, Poland, or Finland, but rather the one posed to Russia itself.

Kaliningrad is likely to remain a problem area for Russia in how to deal with the enclave's sensitive political, economic, and security dimensions. Moscow may continue to use Kaliningrad as a lever employed to political advantage, as for example was the case in 1995 when the Russian government hinted that it might deploy nuclear weapons there if Poland were to be admitted into NATO. Even so, Kaliningrad is more likely to remain a geostrategic liability than an asset to Russia.

Today Kaliningrad is a key residual security challenge for the entire North and Central European region. The very scope of Soviet military deployments there, the environmental degradation, deteriorating social conditions of the population, crime, and the extent of dependence on transit with Russia make Kaliningrad arguably the most enduring security threat to the region for years to come. Those problems are going to become ever more pronounced if Russia continues to move away from democracy and toward greater centralization of its state and political institutions.

THE BALTIC STATES IN THE EU AND NATO

There is no question that in political terms the Baltic states were ready for NATO membership in 2004.[29] Since independence, Estonia, Latvia, and Lithuania have reestablished democratic institutions and created working market economic systems. The three also rank among the most strongly pro-U.S. and generally pro-Western states in the region, and their political elites see membership in NATO as the fulfillment of their national aspirations. Recent history of Soviet occupation and concern over resurgent Russian imperialism figure prominently in Baltic elite security calculations, making territorial defense a priority. At the same time, the Baltics have made a determined effort to restructure their defense in order to contribute to NATO's new missions.

When considering the military potential of the Baltic states in NATO, the relative scale of the question has to be kept in mind. These are small nations, with a combined population of under eight million. Their principal contributions to NATO have been their location, their intelligence and police cooperation, and specialized limited niche military capabilities, such as demining and peace operations. One clear asset that the Baltics as a group have brought to NATO is the Baltic Air Surveillance Network, or the BALTNET project. The system is built around state-of-the art equipment supplied by Lockheed Martin that after enlargement was integrated into the NATO system. BALTNET has enabled Estonia, Latvia, and Lithuania to accelerate their military reform and integration into NATO by laying the groundwork for full interoperability. Drawing on U.S. and European assistance, BALTNET's Regional Airspace Surveillance Coordination Center (RASCC) in Karmelava, Lithuania, was formally inaugurated on June 6, 2000, with the official launching of 24-hour surveillance on January 1, 2001.[30]

In contrast to the BALTNET system, all three Baltic armed forces remain a work in progress. They are conscript-based and still largely in the process of development. The Estonian and Latvian armed forces number about 5,500 each, while the Lithuanian military is approximately 13,500 strong.[31] Estonia and Lithuania have implemented a 2 percent GDP defense budget, but Latvia has lagged behind, with approximately 1.4–1.5 percent of GDP committed to defense in 2002.[32] All three Baltic states have participated in peace support operations and have performed quite well; they also supported U.S. operations in the Middle East. However, their potential contribution should again be kept in the context of the overall size of their armed forces and their limited resources. For example, Estonian participation in the KFOR Multinational Specialized Unit (MSU), part of a NATO-led international force responsible for maintaining security in Kosovo, was limited to the deployment of twenty-one soldiers and an officer assigned to a company of the Italian Carabinieri.[33] Still, participation in peace support operations was important to the development of the armed forces of the Baltic states because it exposed their military personnel to NATO procedures and accelerated their professionalization.

In terms of readily deployable troops, the available Baltic forces are negligible. The Baltic Battalion (BALTBAT), headquartered in Adazi, Latvia, was skeletal as of 2002, with the core staff training to deploy three companies, one from each of the member states, and the proposal was subsequently put on hold. In 2002 plans also called for the creation of three deployable battalions by 2005 (ESTBAT, LATBAT, and LITBAT).[34] Latvia's current 2002–2008 reform program has addressed some of the remaining structural deficiencies. It calls for the establishment of the Joint Headquarters, the Navy Operational Command, the Air Operational Command, and the Special Forces Command. Latvia is also working on a model that would augment the regular armed forces with the National Guard. It stipulates the increase of the peacetime strength of the Latvian armed forces to 7,800 personnel by 2008.[35]

The air forces and air defense capabilities of the three Baltic states are similarly limited, with only a few of the available aircraft and helicopters actually operational. Their role is limited to surveillance, rescue, and some transport duties. However, that is not an area where the Balts can make a meaningful contribution to NATO, nor should they be asked to, as their air-defense assets are better concentrated in BALTNET. The Baltic states can be expected to contribute to peace support operations training at a modest rate. They should also be able to develop specialized capabilities and raise a new generation of senior staff officers to continue the reform process in the region.

Combining resources has been critical to Baltic military modernization. The Baltic Defense College (BALTDEFCOL), set up in 1998 in Tartu, Estonia, with Western support and staffing assistance, has been a success. Estonia, Latvia, and Lithuania have pooled resources to develop a combined mine countermeasures capability within the Baltic Naval Squadron (BALTRON). In addition, the three countries have been working on a mobilization database with the acronym BALTPERS as part of a joint Swedish-Baltic project.[36] Military cooperation among the Baltic states has been augmented by an emerging pattern of interregional cooperation, exemplified by the creation of a joint Lithuanian-Polish unit.

The ongoing restructuring of the Baltic defense establishments following admission to NATO entails both the development of new capabilities and dealing with residual problems from the Soviet era, such as devastated military bases and attendant environmental degradation. So far, Lithuania has achieved the most progress in rebuilding and modernizing the base infrastructure inherited from the Soviet period. Under the leadership of Gen. Jonas Kronkaitis, Lithuania has focused on upgrading its military facilities to create the prerequisites of the Western-type military.[37] However, the equipment used by the Baltic states remains a problem. It is a collection of Swedish, American, Soviet, and Israeli arms, in part purchased and in part received as grants.

Overall, the military capabilities of the Baltic states are limited and will remain so for the foreseeable future. The governments of Estonia, Latvia, and Lithuania have demonstrated their political support for military reform through NATO's Membership Action Plan (MAP) process, but they can only do so much. They were judged successful enough to be admitted to NATO, but in order to become meaningful contributors, the Baltic states need to leverage their assets carefully, including their territory, air-surveillance system, intelligence and police cooperation with NATO, and their specialized niche capabilities, such as demining and peace-support operations.

The three Baltic states have committed to increasing their defense budgets and continued military modernization. In 2004 Estonia created a small reaction force, Lithuania increased its levels of compatibility with NATO and put in place plans to have a NATO-interoperable reaction brigade by 2006 in addition to its joint peacekeeping battalion with Poland, and Latvia established a motorized infantry battalion for NATO missions. Although the scale of the Baltic states' contributions must always be kept in the context of their small size and limited resources, it is indicative of their commitment to NATO that as of 2005 Latvia had developed specialized ordnance and minesweeping units, Estonia was in the process of developing one, while Lithuania was readying a medical unit for NATO operations.[38]

For the Baltic states, the gist of their contribution to NATO has been their location, their intelligence and police cooperation in the war on terrorism, several specialized capabilities, and the BALTNET air-surveillance system. In the final analysis, however, the three can provide only a marginal contribution to NATO's operations. Maintaining defense spending at 2 percent of GDP, while important as a symbol of the Baltic states' commitment to contribute to common defense, will not radically improve their overall capabilities.

On balance, the Baltic enlargement of NATO is important because of its symbolic significance—it erases the remnants of the Cold War division of Europe—and because of its political implications. NATO's willingness to bring in the three former Soviet republics is a reaffirmation of the continued viability of Article X of the North Atlantic Treaty and a significant step toward further integration of the Baltic littoral with the West. Politically, NATO enlargement into the Baltic stands on the merits as an unequivocal and fitting conclusion to the decade of the region's postcommunist transition. Today, the Baltic states are three democracies ready to claim their place in the Euro-Atlantic community.

What remains less obvious is how Baltic membership in NATO will contribute to the already diminished military capabilities of the alliance. Perhaps precisely because the military aspect of NATO has been downgraded, the political payoff of restoring the three Baltic states to the West will ultimately outweigh their limited military contribution. In light of the region's torturous history, however, it begs the question of how much the alliance that Estonia, Latvia, and Lithuania joined in 2004 still has in common with the alliance to which they had once aspired.

REGIONAL SECURITY CALCULUS ALONG THE NORTHEASTERN LITTORAL

Questions about Russia's political evolution remain central to the regional security equation in the eastern Baltic Littoral, and nowhere more clearly than for the three Baltic states, given their history of direct Russian occupation. The Russian question remains very much on the minds of two other regional states as well—Finland and Poland—the former always mindful of the memory of the Winter War and the forced "neutrality" of the Cold War, the latter because of the history of Soviet invasion in 1939, the post–World War II domination by the Soviet Union, and the country's satellite status vis-à-vis Moscow. Although the region has been stabilized in the aftermath of dual enlargement in 2004, the devolution of Russian democracy and the growing pressure from Moscow on Ukraine in the Russian near abroad have raised serious concerns about long-term trends in the Baltic.

Russia factors into the region's security dynamic on several planes; while developing a working cooperative relationship with Russia is the shared interest of all states that now constitute the boundary of the enlarged EU. Relations with Russia will remain a central issue for the EU states in the region, as it touches on their vital security concerns. The region needs Russian cooperation in a variety of areas, from combating international terrorism and crime to energy supply to nonproliferation initiatives. One forum for this is the common regional policy on Russia within the EU, through the so-called "3 plus 3" contacts, or meetings between three Scandinavian EU members and the three

Baltic states, as well as close cooperation with two critical Central European EU states, Germany and Poland. The imperative to develop a coherent policy on cooperation with Russia among the "EU eight" in the Baltic region will be a challenge for the coming years, as each of the countries has a slightly different view on the dangers and opportunities inherent in Russian initiatives.

Relations between the EU Baltic littoral states, especially Estonia, Lithuania, Latvia, Poland, and Finland, will always weigh more heavily on traditionally difficult security considerations, as will the policy of Norway on account of its proximity to Russia. For the border states, Russia will remain the most important military threat in the region, and its traditional military capabilities will continue to be a serious consideration when they structure their defense policies. Finland's decision to balance its growing commitment to international missions with traditionally strong territorial defense and Poland's commitment to retaining a viable territorial defense capability—even as it ventures further afield in international operation—are clear signs that geostrategic considerations remain critical in the region and are likely to define the region's security in traditional terms.

The extent to which regional security will balance between old and new tasks will hinge on domestic political developments in Russia, as well as on the progress of the current Russian military modernization program, to be completed in the 2010s. The residual Russian conventional military capability in the St. Petersburg and Kaliningrad districts will remain a focus of attention for all border EU states, while Poland will focus additional attention on the close ties between Russia and Belarus and, most importantly, on the political evolution of Ukraine. In Polish strategic planning, Ukraine's continued sovereignty and independence from Russia, combined with Kiev's aspirations for NATO and EU membership, are essential components of regional security and stability.

In addition to the Russian residual military presence, the thrust of Russian military reform will be a significant variable in the region's security. Russia's impressive economic performance in 2003 and 2004, especially the windfall for Russia from continuing high oil prices that contributed to a 7.3 percent GDP increase in 2003, freed additional resources for defense. Another sign of change in the Russian economy that has had a direct impact on the future of military modernization has been the increase in machinery and equipment imports; the growth of capital investment in Russia for 2003 was 12.9 percent, compared to 3 percent for 2002. Although in 2004 Russia posted a smaller GDP growth rate of about 5.5 percent overall, in part because of anticipated declines in oil prices, Russia seemed to be on the road to economic recovery as of 2005. The improved economic performance enabled Russia to increase its defense budget, from 262 billion rubles ($8.4 billion) in

2002 to 10.6 billion rubles in 2003 ($10.6 billion) to 411 billion rubles ($30.6 billion) in 2004.[39] All of these statistics could potentially raise the stakes in the Baltic region's security equation.

The past decade saw dramatic reductions in the size of the Russian armed forces, bringing their peacetime strength down from 4.8 million to 1.2 million personnel, and reductions are likely to continue down to 800,000. However, since then Russia has adopted a 2002–2010 modernization and rearmament program, emphasizing R&D in key areas, especially new missile development. On November 17, 2004, President Vladimir Putin announced Russia's determination to develop and deploy a new generation of nuclear missile systems that would, in Putin's words, "surpass those of any other nuclear power."[40] Putin's announcement reflected Russia's continued commitment to nuclear deterrence and delivered a signal that U.S.–led efforts to deploy missile defense systems would not go unanswered. Russia has also strengthened its position as a major weapons exporter, with India and China as its key markets, and is making inroads in southeast Asia and the Middle East. Although as of 2005 it was perhaps premature to speak of Russia's return to a more proactive military stance, the conditions of the Russian military forces had clearly improved relative to the situation in the 1990s.[41]

Perhaps more important to regional security concerns in the Baltic northeast than Russian military modernization itself have been domestic political developments in the Russian Federation, especially the recentralization of the state administration under Putin and growing Russian pressure to reassert Moscow's influence on the near abroad—especially Ukraine. The fall 2004 Ukrainian election, including two visits by Putin in support of the pro-Russian candidate Prime Minister Viktor F. Yanukovich against the pro-Western opposition leader Viktor A. Yushchenko (though ultimately Putin failed to secure Yanukovich's election), was a sign that Russia might be reverting to more proactive and heavy-handed tactics. The growing perception in the region that Putin's particular brand of nationalism will likely define his policies toward the EU, NATO, and the Nordic-Baltic region suggests that the EU frontier states will need to maintain a two-track security policy that, while adapting to the new power-projection requirements of NATO, will retain a viable territorial defense capability until Russia's policy choices become clear.

NOTES

1. Vladimir Shamberg, "Russia in Search of Its Place in the Post–Cold War World," special edition, *Airpower Journal* (1995), at www.airpower.maxwell.af.mil/airchronichles/apj/shamberg/html.

2. Laura Eleonoora Kauppila, "The Baltic Puzzle: Russia's Policy Towards Estonia and Latvia, 1992–1997" (postgraduate thesis, University of Helsinki, 1999), 2.

3. *Obwód kaliningradzki w kontekście rozszerzenia Unii Europejskiej* [The Kaliningrad District in the context of the enlargement of the European Union] (Warsaw: Osrodek Studiów Wschodnich, July 2001).

4. Evgeny Vinokurov, "Economic Prospects for Kaliningrad Between the EU Enlargement and Russia's Integration Into the World Economy" (working document 201, Center for European Policy Studies, Brussels, 2004), 1.

5. Natalia Smorodinskaya, "Kaliningrad's Economic Growth Problem," in *Russia and the European Union*, ed. Oksana Antonenko and Karen Pinnick, 263–276 (London: Routledge, 2004).

6. Kauppila, 4.

7. Kauppila, 10.

8. Kauppila, 13.

9. Kauppila, 2.

10. Kauppila, 20.

11. Kauppila, 22.

12. *Obwód kaliningradzki.*

13. *Pravda,* "Federation Council Speaker: Baltic Fleet Is Weighty Argument in Russia's Negotiations with Europe Over EU and NATO," September 9, 2002, english .pravda.ru/politics/2002/09/09/36204.html.

14. Roger McDermott, "Historic Russia-NATO Maneuvers," *Eurasia Daily Monitor* 1, no. 70, August 10, 2004, www.jamestown.org/publications_details.php? volume_id=401&issue_id=3043&article_id=2368385.

15. GlobalSecurity.org, "Kaliningrad Special Defense District (KOOR)," KOOR GlobalSecurity.org, March 8, 2004, www.globalsecurity.org/military/world/russia/ KOOR-kaliningrad.htm.

16. *Obwód kaliningradzki.*

17. Klaus Carsten Pedersen, "Kaliningrad: Armed Forces and Mission," in *Kaliningrad: The European Amber Region*, ed. Pertti Joenniemi and Jan Prawitz (Aldershot, UK: Ashgate Publishing 1998), 107.

18. Pedersen, "Kaliningrad," 109.

19. During an interview following his summit with President George W. Bush in Bratislava on February 26, 2005, Russia's President Vladimir Putin acknowledged that the Baltic states had a valid historical grievance against Russia.

20. Institute of Strategic Stability, "Transcript of Press Conference for Russian and Foreign Media by Russian Minister of Foreign Affairs Sergey Lavrov Following Informal Meeting of the Russia-NATO Council's Foreign Ministers: Statement of Russia's Ministry of Foreign Affairs," April 5, 2004, at www.iss.niiit.ru/sobdog-e/ sd-168.htm.

21. Reuters, "Russia Proposes NATO-Compatible Peacekeeping Force," February 10, 2005.

22. Arkady Moshes, "EU Enlargement in the Baltic Sea Region and Russia: Obvious Problems, Unclear Solutions" (PONARS policy memo 171, Institute of Europe, Center for Strategic & International Studies, Washington, DC, 2000).

23. Evgeny Vinokurov, "Kaliningrad's Borders and Transit to Mainland Russia: Practicalities and Remaining Bottlenecks" (Brussels: Centre for European Policy Studies, 2005), www.ceps.be/Article.php?article_id=264&.

24. Vinokurov, "Kaliningrad's Borders and Transit to Mainland Russia."

25 Valentinas Mite, "Russia/EU: New Travel Rules Begin for Kaliningrad, With Only Minor Hitches Reported," *Radio Free Europe/Radio Liberty*, July 1, 2003, www.globalsecurity.org/military/library/news/2003/07/mil-030701-rfel-155533.htm.

26. "EU-Russia Cooperation Programme/TACIS Russia," *The European Commission's Delegation to Russia*, n.d., at www.delrus.cec.eu.int/en/p_260.htm.

27. Association of International Experts on the Development of the Kaliningrad Region, *EU-Russia Partnership on Kaliningrad*, Moscow: MEMO2/02/169, July 12, 2002, at kaliningradexpert.org/stuff/docs/EU-Russia Partnership on Kaliningrad_eng.doc.

28. Ingmar Olderg, "Kaliningrad: Problems and Prospects," in *Kaliningrad: The European Amber Region*, 3.

29. This section includes material published by the author in the summer 2004 issue of *Orbis*. See: Andrew A. Michta, "Central Europe and the Baltic Littoral in NATO," *Orbis*, Summer 2004, 409–421.

30. *Baltic Defense Co-operation*, 15.

31. Christopher Langton, ed., *The Military Balance 2002–2003* (London: International Institute for Strategic Studies, 2002). The figures provided by IISS are not always in line with the figures reported by the countries themselves. For example, Lithuanian Ministry of Defense (MOD) sources put the total number of the Lithuanian armed forces personnel at approximately 12,000.

32. The quoted defense spending for Latvia is my estimate. The official figure supplied by the Latvian government for 2002 is the plan to spend 1.75 percent of GDP (90.95 million Latvian lats), with the projected figure for 2003 at 2.00 percent of GDP (LVL113.15 million). However, the 2002 budget allocated to the Ministry of Defense was 68.79 million LVL, which (although according to the government marks a 43-percent increase over the 2001 budget) would still fall short of the planned 1.75-percent figure. For the official Latvian numbers on defense spending, see *Latvian Republic Defence Budget for Year 2002*, at www.mod.gov.lv/index.php?pid=1220.

33. NATO and International Organisations Department, Ministry of Defence, Republic of Estonia, *Estonia and International Peace Operations* (Tallinn: NATO and International Organisations Department, Ministry of Defence, Republic of Estonia, 2002), 8.

34. Briefing at the Estonian Ministry of Defense, May 13, 2002.

35. Briefing at the Latvian Ministry of Defense, Riga, Latvia, May 15, 2002.

36. Briefing at the Latvian Ministry of Defense.

37. Briefing by Gen. Jonas Kronkaitis at the Lithuanian Ministry of Defense, Vilnius, Lithuania, May 17, 2002.

38. George C. Marshall European Center for Security Studies, "Dual Enlargement and the Baltic States: Security Policy Implications" (report of the George C. Marshall Center for Security Studies Conference, Tallinn, Estonia, February 11–13, 2004).

39. Christopher Langton, ed., *The Military Balance 2004–2005* (London: International Institute for Strategic Studies, 2004), 294.

40. Steven Lee Myers, "Putin Says New Missile Systems Will Give Russia a Nuclear Edge," *The New York Times*, international section, November 18, 2004.

41. For a review of the record of Russian military modernization in the 1990s, see Roger N. McDermott, "Putin's Military Priorities: Modernizing the Armed Forces," in *Russian Military Reform 1992–2002*, ed. Anne C. Aldis and Roger N. McDermott, 259–277 (Portland, OR: Frank Cass Publishers, 2003).

· 5 ·

American Policy toward North and Central Europe before and after September 11, 2001

FROM 1997 MADRID TO THE "MAGNIFICENT SEVEN"

$\mathscr{I}$n the 1990s NATO enlargement policy became the centerpiece of the United States' relations with postcommunist democracies in Central Europe and the Baltic littoral. The first round of enlargement, completed in 1999, would frame the direction of NATO's evolution. The process of enlargement raised the question of the long-term viability of NATO as a defensive alliance, as well as concerns about NATO's place in regional security when compared to the EU's Security and Defense Policy, especially the extent to which the ESDP would eventually compete with NATO.[1] The debates that accompanied the process of NATO enlargement and the relationship between NATO and the nascent European security identity reflected not just the ongoing evolution of the alliance itself but also a change in transatlantic relations. For the United States, NATO enlargement became a vehicle for fostering stability in the region through conditionality and external norm setting.

NATO enlargement proceeded during the time of equally radical change within the European Union, as the Continent's integration project moved to the next level of monetary and political union, culminating in 2004 with the addition of ten new members. In north and central Europe, it was apparent in the 1990s that the dual NATO and EU enlargement might generate at least as much strain as synergy and that the two organizations might at times work at cross-purposes. For Poland and the Baltic states, security in relations with Russia would never be considered adequate if the alliance arrangements did not include American commitment to the region. For the Nordic countries, the extent of their commitment to NATO would be defined by the nature of their Cold War security cooperation with the United States—inside or outside the alliance—as well as their views on the residual value of NATO for their security. For Germany, NATO was inextricably tied to Berlin's view of its own history, its geostrategic position, the future role of the European Union, and German-Russian relations.

From the start of NATO's enlargement into Central Europe and the Baltic littoral, the United States would encounter in the region a diversity of official views on its role and on NATO's future mission. American policy would drive the evolution of NATO to a much greater extent than the policies of any of the other members of the alliance, but transatlanticism after the Cold War would be progressively checked by the pull of the Continental security option. Even before the trauma of the September 11 terrorist attack against the United States, Washington's priorities and the focus of its security policy were shifting to Asia and the Middle East to a degree never experienced during the Cold War. Also, the overall benign security environment in Europe following the disintegration of the Warsaw Pact—the Balkan wars notwithstanding—had a different impact on the countries in the region: For some it reaffirmed their European identity; for others it strengthened their commitment to transatlanticism. The policy of enlargement reflected the expectations that the norm-setting aspect of the alliance and the emphasis on NATO as a community of values would suffice to reconstitute and sustain it as a viable security organization into the twenty-first century.

The United States' decision to support NATO enlargement into Central Europe was decisive in helping overcome the divisions of the Cold War era. The 1997 NATO Madrid summit invitation to Poland, Hungary, and the Czech Republic to join the alliance and their subsequent admission in 1999 established several precedents that would define the future of the alliance. First, by emphasizing the political dimension of enlargement and deemphasizing the persistent problems of capabilities and interoperability, Washington sent the first signal that the center of gravity in the alliance had begun to shift from the military to the political aspects of NATO. That shift in emphasis within the alliance was the beginning of a more profound transformation of American policy toward Europe. Although in the aftermath of the 1999 enlargement concern over the devolution of NATO and its transformation into a collective security organization would be raised in different forums, the Clinton administration seemed unable to come to grips with the long-term consequences for the alliance of the progressive degeneration of its military capabilities.

In terms of military modernization, the record of the 1999 NATO enlargement into Central Europe has been mixed. In Poland, Hungary, and the Czech Republic, the record of success in force reduction and institutional restructuring has been offset by persistent problems in equipment, modernization, and readiness. If anything, the record of the 1999 entrants shows that the cycle of reductions may have reached the point of diminishing returns and that serious problems continue to lie ahead unless there is a commitment in Central Europe to replenish and rebuild forces. The backsliding on reform in Hungary, the implosion of the Czech reform program (albeit for reasons outside the government's control), and the uneven record of military reform in Poland suggest that modernization may reach only a part of their armed forces. In effect that would create "two militaries" in Central Europe: a small, better equipped and NATO-compatible force capable of participating in alliance missions, and the residual force with deteriorating equipment and readiness levels. Whether such a model is sustainable in the long run without creating serious morale problems among the military remains to be seen. The successive MAP cycles after 1999 were intended to correct the problems of longtime military weakness of the incoming allies with the next trench of entrants. Though in some areas they made the Baltic states more adapted overall in the military sphere than the 1999 entrants, the cycles failed to change Washington's view that NATO was becoming first and foremost a political tool.

At its most basic level, NATO enlargement benefited the United States because it added new allies that would be decisively pro-American in their outlook for the foreseeable future. Preserving NATO preserved American leverage in Europe and continued to emphasize the special position of the United States in transatlantic relations. The experience of the Kosovo campaign confirmed the U.S. view that NATO had lost its marginal military utility and that when fighting an out-of-area war the alliance might in fact constitute a hindrance. Kosovo exposed glaring deficiencies in the capabilities of the European allies, and not just in the new 1999 entrants, although their problems remained the most severe. In Kosovo, the U.S. military sustained the bulk of the war burden, including intelligence, logistics, airpower, ordnance, and command and control. The notorious "war by committee" image of NATO's Kosovo campaign became the lasting legacy of that war.[2] Kosovo is likely to go down in the history of the alliance as the landmark campaign that would set the course of NATO's devolution in the twenty-first century.

A decisive shift in 2001 in U.S. policy on NATO enlargement marked a turning point for the alliance's transformation into a predominantly political organization with limited military capabilities. In his speech on June 15, 2001, at Warsaw University on an official visit to Poland, President George W. Bush outlined his broad vision of a new security community. As he put it, "all of Europe's new democracies, from the Baltic to the Black Sea and all that lie between, should have the same chance for security and freedom—and the same chance to join the institutions of Europe—as Europe's old democracies have." Pledging "no more Munichs" and "no more Yaltas," President Bush spoke of his belief in "NATO membership for all of Europe's democracies that seek it and are ready to share the responsibilities that NATO brings."[3]

The president's speech was instrumental in setting aside the debates that followed the 1999 round of NATO enlargement, focusing on the core issue of the new members' capabilities and ways to avoid the repetition of the problems of 1999 in the subsequent enlargement cycle. The Bush decision went beyond the transformation that NATO had undergone in the run-up to the 1999 enlargement. In part it was due to the recognition that *defense* and *security* were no longer synonymous as they had been in the Cold War, and that threats to Europe would be predominantly internal. Between the 1999 enlargement and the Bush Warsaw speech, it remained an open question for future U.S. security whether NATO enlargement would repeat the entirely political decision that drove the 1999 round or military considerations would be restored.[4]

The British in particular were preoccupied during that time with focusing the next round of enlargement on the continued military capabilities of the new entrants.[5] The British were concerned that if the necessary reforms were not made prior to extending the invitation, the subsequent round of enlargement would repeat the experience of the Polish, Czech, and Hungarian cases, whereby promises of military modernization were left unfilled. The British preference, in line with some American observers, was to rely on the "regatta approach," with all candidates being offered a broad invitation but new members being admitted on a case-by-case basis, according as they met the political and military criteria.[6] The MAP process might have been such a mechanism for identifying and verifying the criteria.

Throughout the pre-enlargement debate, the Baltic states were a political tipping point. In contrast to expansion in the southerly direction, NATO's decision not to enlarge into the Baltic region would in effect redline the region, giving Russia the implicit prerogative to decide the framework of the security of Estonia, Latvia, and Lithuania.[7] That was not just the view of the Americans or the British, but it also reflected regional consensus in the Baltic region. For example, while the Finns showed precious little interest in joining NATO, their government officials privately expressed the view that they could not imagine the second round of NATO enlargement without the Baltics. Among the Nordic members of NATO, Denmark was the strongest proponent of including the Baltic states, especially Lithuania, in the second round of enlargement.[8] Regardless of the permutations and the numbers of the potential Baltic entrants in the second round, there was by late 2001 an apparent consensus in both Washington and Brussels that at least one Baltic state needed to be included in the upcoming enlargement. It was then the logical extension of the argument that if one Baltic state were to join NATO, the political price in terms of potential tensions with Russia made the membership for all three a logical choice.

By the time NATO was deciding on the next round of enlargement, several aspects of the alliance were clearly showing the core trends in its evolution, as well as its major limitations. First, the upcoming second round of NATO enlargement brought the organization of the headquarters and the standard operating procedures up for revision, as function began to outstrip practice. An increased number of members would increase the difficulty of NATO's day-to-day operations. An ancillary issue, though related to the overall functioning of the headquarters, was the question of decision-making procedures and ways to reach consensus on policy, so that NATO could actually act in a crisis. It was also clear that, in addition to focusing on additional nonmilitary threats, NATO needed to review the workings of its military commands, as well as its force structures, with an eye to greater specialization as part of defense reform.

President George W. Bush's June 2001 Warsaw speech ended the argument about the possible permutations of the enlargement process. The September 11 attacks and the U.S. decision to pass on NATO as the formula for the Afghanistan campaign imposed the key limitation on NATO's utility as a military organization. The seven new invitees were brought into NATO in 2004 as another wave, this time even more problematic than the 1999 one had been: all of them, with the possible exception of Romania, were small states. They accounted for seven votes in the North Atlantic Council (NAC) but offered only marginal military capabilities. That, in combination with the widening capabilities gap between the United States and Europe after September 11, would raise the question of whether consensus building was still the workable formula for Washington's interaction with NATO members.

In hindsight, it is clear that when in June 2001 in Warsaw President George W. Bush announced his vision for enlarged NATO stretching between the Baltic and the Black Sea he set the alliance on the road to becoming "political NATO." The rhetoric of the moment aside, the Bush redefinition meant that NATO would now serve three functions: (1) continuing to channel American influence in Europe, (2) offering a preferred alternative to a bilateral U.S.–EU relationship as the foundation of transatlantic relations, and (3) a continued "socializing" capability to the transformation of the postcommunist states and tying them to the larger community of democratic nations.

After September 11 the first function would be augmented by a new emphasis on strengthening bilateral ties between the United States and its closest supporters in NATO, with a view toward tapping the alliance for "coalitions of the willing" in the war against terrorism. The Bush administration's policy on enlargement was that Washington would support a large group of new members, with the subsequent invitation to seven applicants to join the alliance. An important change after the September 11 attack was a new relationship of cooperation in the war on terrorism between the United States and Russia. In 2004 the largest single group ever to join NATO was brought onboard, extending NATO into the Baltic region as well as bringing Romania and Bulgaria—the two states that prior to September 11 had limited prospects of making it into that round of enlargement—into the alliance.

The scope of the 2004 enlargement was significant because it suggested that the United States had by then conceded that the near-term military capabilities of the new allies would be limited, perhaps marginal; instead, it focused on the political and norm-setting dimensions of enlargement. It also made a clear statement as to which kinds of support capabilities the new members possessed would be most valued in Washington. The political dimension of enlargement did not completely come to the fore until the 2003 transatlantic break over Iraq. American support for the inclusion of Romania and Bulgaria could have been seen as a signal that the two countries' participation in the stability operations in Afghanistan, including the deployment of a contingent of Romanian combat troops after the overthrow of the Taliban, would be considered an important test of their support for the United States.

The developments following September 11, 2001, in particular the U.S. campaigns in Afghanistan and Iraq, made the debates of NATO's role largely moot. They rephrased the core question not of whether NATO or the ESDP would provide the preferred formula for European security, but rather how to adjust American-European relations to the gradual decline of the former and the continual marginal utility of the latter. The most critical development was Washington's decision to pursue the Afghanistan military campaign against al Qaeda and the Taliban outside NATO's framework. The prevailing view among some of the most seasoned international staff at NATO headquarters at the time was that NATO did not take a decisive role in Afghanistan because the United States simply did not push for it.[9]

American reluctance to engage NATO militarily in Afghanistan was not just a matter of choosing to go it alone so as to retain maximum flexibility, although that was a consideration. A significant part of the problem was that during the 1990s NATO enlarged by pursuing the normative political track but proved much less capable of reforming its military side. In terms of defense capabilities, NATO's questionable value to the United States after September 11 reflected the fact that it retained the military structures of the Cold War era: The out-of-area Kosovo operation seemed to have failed to generate sufficient pressure for reform. From the U.S. vantage point, until the Europeans rethink how their forces are structured, the "usability" issue will remain.

BETWEEN NATO AND THE ESDP

The announcement by President George W. Bush in August 2004 that in the coming decade the United States would pull seventy thousand troops, mostly out of Europe, for redeployment at home, in Turkey, and in some of the former communist states of central and southeastern Europe was an unmistakable sign that NATO's military identity was undergoing a profound transformation. It continued the hollowing-out of NATO that had been under way since the 1999 enlargement cycle. It was also another indicator that the break in German–U.S. relations over the Second Iraq War was more deeply rooted and more enduring than many had first thought, setting the framework for a new pattern of transatlantic relations. The Schröder government and the German public recognized that the decision to pull two U.S. divisions out of Germany would go far beyond the economic impact on the affected communities. Defense Minister Peter Struck spoke not just for the government but also for a large segment of the German population when he expressed a general sense of regret following the U.S. announcement of the troop withdrawal.[10] Notwithstanding the fact that the redeployment plans had been in the works for several years, it was impossible for the Germans to escape the symbolism of the American announcement as marking the end of an era. It also renewed focus on the idea of building a new EU-based European security system.

It remains the subject of debate when exactly the discussion about a European security system within NATO evolved in the direction of the idea of an autonomous European defense capability. As early as 1998 the evolution of ESDI (European Security and Defense Identity) within NATO, in combination with the CJTF (Combined Joint Task Forces) concept that was to strengthen NATO, gave way to a crucial step toward EU autonomy on security issues: the European Security and Defense Policy (ESDP). The idea for ESDP was launched in the wake of the December 1998 St. Malo initiative by British Prime Minister Tony Blair and French President Jacques Chirac, followed by NATO's 1999 war in Kosovo. Formally announced by the European Council in Cologne in June 1999, the ESDP set up a new institutional framework, including the High Representative for the Common Foreign and Security Policy (CFSP); a Political and Security Committee (French acronym COPS) consisting of senior officials from each EU member state and charged with monitoring crisis situations and advising the European Council on possible solutions; a European Union Military Committee (EUMC), the highest EU military body composed of the chiefs of the defense staffs of member states; and a European Union Military Staff (EUMS) to work under the military direction of the EUMC.[11] These institutions were formally launched in December 1999 at the European Council meeting in Helsinki, which also established the military "Headline Goal" of creating a corps-size force of sixty thousand troops capable of rapid deployment in sixty days and sustainable for one year to deploy for significant humanitarian, crisis-management, and even peace-enforcement operations. The force was to be ready by December 2003 and was to enable the EU to conduct EU-led military operations with or without recourse to NATO assets, as well as to fully contribute to

NATO-led operations.[12] St. Malo and the follow-on Helsinki meeting were landmarks in EU–U.S. relations.

The further hollowing-out of NATO in the wake of the war in Kosovo shifted the focus of debate on European security toward the ESDP. Kosovo's role in giving a new impetus for the development of the ESDP cannot be overstated. It marked a glaring recognition on the part of the Europeans and the Americans of how far apart they were in terms of both their military capabilities and their thinking about strategy and the proper venues for the application of military power. Further differences emerged on the direction and process of the second round of NATO enlargement, as well as a host of other political issues, from the Kyoto Protocol to the International Criminal Court to the ABM Treaty and missile defense.

The first round of NATO enlargement focused on the ability of the new entrants to be politically effective within the alliance. Hence, the conditionality that guided the process focused on civilian democratic control over the military and institutional transformation of the defense structure. The political impact of enlargement both internally on the candidate countries and externally on regional security configuration, including the reaction of Russia, had been at the center of the process leading up to the 1997 Madrid invitation. Another important consideration was the question of the new entrants' political reliability—a question that proved pertinent when the alliance went to war in Kosovo in 1999. During the Kosovo operation, Poland passed the test with flying colors, Hungary's performance was acceptable, and the Czech Republic needed considerable pressure to meet the test. Finally, the assumption was that once the political criteria were met, the new members would proceed with the required military transformation. While overall worries about reliability and political competence were ultimately proven to be unfounded, military modernization remained a serious problem.

The attacks of September 11 created the last opportunity to revitalize the Atlantic alliance within existing structural frameworks of NATO. Despite the invocation of Article 5 by NATO, apparently on the initiative of Tony Blair, the United States and its European allies remained polarized on the very conceptualization of the new international security environment. While the Americans spoke of the Global War on Terrorism (GWOT) as framed by the highly moral definition of the struggle of good versus evil, the Europeans emphasized the political dimension of the problem, police and intelligence cooperation, as well as the root causes of the conflict, including the Israeli-Palestinian conflict. Likewise, the disarray within the EU and the growing tensions between the large, medium, and small members of the EU added another wrinkle of European disunity to the highly charged issue of whether the EU and American security policies would align in this new global struggle.

The invocation of Article 5 was perhaps the last opportunity for NATO to remake itself as a meaningful military organization, and will likely be viewed in hindsight as the swan song of the alliance. On September 21, 2001, the European Council held an extraordinary meeting that, while expressing "total support" for the American people and recognizing that UN Security Council resolution 1368 made a U.S. military retaliation "legitimate," also outlined a broad European agenda to create the "broadest possible global coalition against terrorism under United Nations aegis." The Europeans emphasized the need to reactivate the Middle East peace process on the basis of the Mitchell and Tenet reports and the "integration of all countries into a fair world system of security, prosperity, and improved development."[13]

At that critical juncture, the United States and the European Union were speaking on the same subject but with different voices. The EU focused on humanitarian relief for Afghanistan and neighboring countries as its first priority. Europe's ESDP leaders embarked on a series of diplomatic visits to central Asia, south Asia, and the Middle East. That series of initiatives was accompanied by greater EU activism in the Mediterranean, toward Turkey, and toward Russia. The Euro-Mediterranean Conference of foreign ministers (November 5–6, 2001) highlighted cooperation and shared goals in the area of economic development, antiterrorism, cultural exchange, and security. In an apparent breakthrough, in early December 2001, Turkey announced its willingness to work with the ESDP.

The greatest weakness of the ESDP has been its military capability. Although at the Capabilities Improvement Conference, held on November 19, 2001, the EU began to address the issue of its deficiencies in the military sphere, progress has been inadequate. For the future of transatlantic relations, the dwindling U.S. capabilities available to Europe, compounded by the inadequacy of the ESDP resources, which are unlikely to be achieved in the coming or even next two decades, have further strained the relationship. That has had a decisive impact on the evolution of bilateral and regional security relations in North and Central Europe.

The decision announced in Prague in 2002 to enlarge NATO by seven new members began the final stage in the process of transforming NATO from a collective defense into a collective security organization. It also reflected a much more profound parting of ways, or to put it differently, the decoupling of Europe and the United States that had taken root in the aftermath of the Kosovo campaign. Kosovo showed, as Frédéric Bozo has observed, that unless the relationship was "rebalanced," the disequilibrium in military capabilities between Europe and the United States, inherited from the Cold War, was no longer tenable.[14] That rebalancing has failed to take place. From the vantage point of smaller powers, specifically the North and

Central Europeans, Kosovo demonstrated how thin the European capabilities to deploy and sustain forces outside the national territory really were, notwithstanding the rhetoric of the June 1992 Petersberg tasks about peace-supporting missions as one of the primary goals of the EU.

THE IMPACT OF AFGHANISTAN AND THE GWOT

The official argument as to why Washington chose not to use NATO as the vehicle for Operation Enduring Freedom is on the surface quite straightforward: the available allied structures were incompatible with the mission at hand.[15] The operation was run by the Central Command outside the area of SHAPE's (Supreme Headquarters Allied Powers Europe) responsibility, and it would have been quite difficult for SHAPE to liaison effectively with CENTCOM. In contrast, the European Command was firmly embedded in the countries for which it had responsibility and had a well-developed system of liaison officers in place. But more than the institutional constraints, the problem was one of the paucity of useful European military capabilities available for Afghanistan. Defense Secretary Donald Rumsfeld's argument that the "mission defines the coalition," which soon became synonymous with the subsequent Iraq operation, was very much at the center of the planning process. As the Bush Administration launched the Global War on Terrorism (GWOT), it insisted on complete operational control of the campaign, asking its allies and partners to contribute only where American plans could be augmented with their capabilities but giving them little influence on the planning process. In short, the United States refused to engage NATO in Afghanistan in a way that would make the September 12, 2001, invocation of Article 5 meaningful beyond its symbolism.

On October 7, 2001, the United States launched Operation Enduring Freedom. Hindsight demonstrates that it marked the end of NATO as a premier transatlantic security organization not only because of the U.S. decision to go it alone but also because during the 1990s NATO never went beyond Europe as the legitimate area of its operations. Although it subsequently provided a small stabilization force for Afghanistan, it would prove crippling to the alliance's prospects that in the fall of 2001 NATO lacked a global definition for its operations. After the 1999 Kosovo operation NATO had engaged in a debate on the meaning of "out-of-area" operations, but at the time it had failed to reach an agreement on how far the geographic area would extend. Instead, decisions about the area would continue to be made as the crises presented themselves, but NATO failed to accept the global scope of operations. The Balkan operations were not conceived as a precedent for operations outside Europe, and NATO's stability operations in Afghanistan were not taken to prove the alliance's readiness to deploy in the Middle East or North Africa. Since there was a lack of such a consensus at the time of the Afghanistan operation, the frequent assertions in Europe about NATO's shared mission did not have real substance. Consensus on the mission at the core meant consensus on the area of NATO's operations and responsibility, and that was still lacking.

For more than a decade prior to the September 11 terrorist attacks on the World Trade Center and the Pentagon, NATO had been looking for a new mission. On September 11 that mission found NATO; Operation Enduring Freedom would test whether a new transatlantic consensus on the mission would emerge or NATO would become progressively irrelevant. The failure to make the first campaign of America's Global War on Terrorism NATO's campaign proved to be a landmark shift. Instead of restoring the transatlantic link, the operation in Afghanistan threatened to decouple America from Europe. It also was a clear sign that, at least going into the Afghan operation, the European members of NATO had not come to grips with the realities of asymmetric warfare as the principal challenge facing the alliance from that time on.

In part NATO's inability to respond forcefully to September 11 was due to the residual structural problem of the alliance inherited from the Cold War era, when defense meant first and foremost deterrence and when NATO was preparing structures that were to be filled up in case of war. That had two consequences: (1) that these structures were by definition larger than required in peacetime, and (2) that few of those units were actually ready to fight on a short notice in the kind of action that would be required after September 11. Such a legacy meant that, as the United States geared up for the Afghan operation, the Europeans were faced with the task of rethinking how their forces were structured and how they spent money on defense. It was a Europe-wide problem, not just limited to NATO members. For example, although during the Cold War Sweden maintained high defense budgets, in 2001 it would have been hard-pressed to deploy more than a battalion out of area.

Operation Enduring Freedom also set the stage for the second round of enlargement in 2004 by outlining the parameters on the practical, if limited, contribution that the prospective new allies could make to the Global War on Terrorism. That in part settled the issue of the Baltic states' membership, as they offered potential staging areas, ports, and additional surveillance capabilities, especially in the area of intelligence and police cooperation. The post–September 11 environment and the run-up to the Afghanistan operation also dramatically changed the prospects for NATO membership of Romania and Bulgaria, as they were now viewed as important staging areas in the war against terrorism, and even more importantly because of their proximity to Turkey, a key U.S. ally in the region.[16] Moreover, both Romania and Bulgaria "earned" their right to become members in the eyes of Washington by contributing forces to the Afghan operation, including a Romanian contingent of several hundred troops and a Bulgarian support unit.

On one level, Operation Enduring Freedom and NATO's ISAF deployment marked the boundaries of NATO's practical contribution to the Bush administration's Global War on Terrorism. On another, it marked the continued commitment to the political dimension of the alliance as a useful vehicle for America's influence in Europe that would be infinitely preferable to a bilateral NATO-EU relationship, as it would entail a considerable loss of leverage. NATO has also allowed the United States to develop a new set of bilateral relations between Washington and individual members of the European Union.

2003 IRAQ AND THE UNITED STATES–GERMAN RIFT

No crisis exposed the limitations of post–Cold War NATO more than the transatlantic diplomatic collision over the United States' decision to intervene in Iraq in 2003. Discrepancies over threat perception between the United States and its traditional European allies proved critical for NATO's future as a viable alliance. Although one could argue that Afghanistan need not to have been necessarily viewed as an indicator of where the alliance was heading because of the need to improvise on short notice, Iraq became an all-out test of NATO's internal consensus. While the Europeans accepted the general political tenets of America's GWOT, they were not positioned to act globally if that meant moving their forces to face threats head-on. Another limitation Afghanistan exposed was the need for the European NATO members to move from deterrent to deployable forces and capabilities that would be relevant to the current American goals in the war on terror. What Afghanistan demonstrated was that the question was not whether NATO was becoming more a political than military organization, but rather whether both the Americans and the Europeans both saw the alliance as still vitally relevant to their security needs and their current security situation—the implication being that if allies began to see NATO as no longer relevant to their needs, the alliance would progressively atrophy.

The centerpiece of NATO's crisis in the run-up to the Iraq war was the confrontation over Turkey's invocation of Article 4 of the Washington Treaty as a means of ensuring against eventual retaliation against Turkey by Iraq in the course of the operation. The decision of the French and Belgian governments to block such a decision effectively paralyzed NATO and was a shot across the bow of the alliance. The February 2003 confrontation in the alliance was arguably the worst crisis in the alliance's fifty-three-year history. France, Germany, and Belgium effectively vetoed a plan that would have given Turkey access to defensive equipment, including surveillance aircraft, missile systems, and units trained to deal with biological and chemical attacks to be made available in case Iraq made a retaliatory attack against Turkey. The fact that sixteen of the nineteen members of the alliance had approved the plan raised the question of the viability of consensus as the core criterion for NATO decision making. Since Turkey's request was made in the course of an extraordinary meeting invoked under Article 4, the Franco-German-Belgian decision to block the request sent shock waves across the alliance as well as the candidate countries. In effect, the crisis disclosed the fundamental flaw in the assumption during the 1990s that Article 4 rather than Article 5 would constitute the core of NATO operations. The crisis over Turkey's request under Article 4 raised the real fear that a member requesting assistance in light of its assessment that its security was threatened would not receive support under Article 4 unless all members agreed that such security concerns were real.

What made the February 2003 crisis over Turkey's Article 4 request especially difficult was that the veto was cast by France, Germany, and Belgium as a part of the transatlantic policy quarrel between them and the United States over the American decision to go to war. The dissenting governments argued that while they agreed in principle, they did not want to prejudice the chances for a political solution to the crisis. In effect, NATO decision making was paralyzed because of a fundamental policy disagreement on a request by an individual member state, which should have been treated procedurally as a matter of treaty requirement and not political debate. If NATO were to prove incapable of providing defensive equipment to a member that had requested such assistance, what then was the ultimate validity of the security guarantee under the Washington Treaty? Moreover, the equipment Turkey requested was strictly defensive in nature, which meant a credible case that it would have been used in the campaign against Iraq was difficult to make.

In effect, having failed to participate in the initial combat phase of Operation Enduring Freedom in Afghanistan, NATO was now proving unable to even engage in contingency planning as requested by one of its members. Never before had NATO faced such a question of its credibility, and that had an impact on the debates on military modernization and specialization and the drive to develop niche capabilities. Would smaller states, having substantially refocused their military away from territorial defense, find themselves in a situation where their requests for contingency planning under threat could be blocked by another member state? The heated arguments among the ambassadors as the crisis unfolded, as well as the less-than-diplomatic comments by R. Nicholas Burns, U.S. Permanent Representative to NATO, about a "near death experience" for the alliance,[17] or NATO Secretary General Lord Robertson's assertion that the serious damage was still "above the waterline,"[18] indicated how critical that issue was for NATO's continued viability. For the current and future members in North and Central Europe and the Baltic littoral, the crisis over Turkey became the litmus test of NATO's credibility and its ultimate value to their security.

The crisis over Turkey began the progressive polarization within the alliance that would ultimately result in the Bush Administration's characterization of "old Europe" versus "new Europe." It also placed Germany and Poland on opposite sides of the issue—a clear policy choice for the first time since the two countries had begun cooperating in the 1990s. Marek Siwiec, the head of Poland's National Security Bureau (BBN) and national security adviser to President Aleksander Kwaśniewski, echoed the American view when he charged that the Franco-German-Belgian position was equivalent to supporting Saddam Hussein. The crisis was further aggravated when, after the open letters in support of American policy were published in the *Wall Street Journal*, French President Jacques Chirac asserted that the small new democracies in Central and Eastern Europe should have learned when to sit down and be quiet, insinuating that their support for the United States might endanger their prospects for membership in the European Union.

The crisis was eventually averted by procedural means, in a face-saving move that took the decision out of the NAC. But the damage was done, and it would continue to undercut the allied consensus and NATO's long-term viability. Germany's opposition to Turkey's request was critical in this case— much more so than the position taken by France, which had a long history of discord with the United States. The German position was truly a revolutionary development. In contrast to its nonparticipation in the combat operations of the 1991 Gulf War, where the government asserted that constitutional constraints prevented Germany from taking part, here Berlin simply argued that the problem should be dealt with in a different way.[19] In effect, Germany not only opposed the United States within NATO, but also took a position that was shared not only by France but by Russia and China as well.

The diplomatic clash between the United States and Germany over Iraq made the future of NATO a central issue. The dilemma of the transatlantic crisis was compounded by the fact that since NATO's invocation of Article 5 in the aftermath of the September 11 attack on the World Trade Center, the Europeans had been officially engaged on the side of the United States in the war against international terrorism. Both Washington and Berlin recognized the imperative of rebuilding the transatlantic relationship, but the reality on the ground in Iraq shortly became a major obstacle to that. While it was possible for the German government to engage in the reconstruction of Iraq and the entire region, despite the overwhelming public opposition to the war itself, the rapidly deteriorating situation on the ground in Iraq made such participation impossible. Germany did attempt to leverage its relationship with Iran as the European Union tried to induce Teheran to disavow its nuclear program, but that initiative, though appreciated in Washington, sidestepped the core issue of Iraq.

Iraq suspended the German-American relationship at the highest level, but it did not destroy it. Working relationships below the top political level remained strong, and cooperation continued. Still, the anger and recriminations from the run-up to the war soured the relationship, and the 2004 U.S. presidential campaign intensified the Bush administration's focus on the lack of German support for the Iraq war. In the larger context of the transatlantic relationship, the Iraq war marked post–Cold War Germany's long-anticipated "coming into its own" on foreign policy. What few had expected prior to the second Iraq war was that Berlin would assert its position on foreign policy not alongside America but rather in opposition to it. Allegiance to the United States has been considered since World War II to be the core foundation of German security policy, a view shared in the pre-2004 European Union by the United Kingdom and Denmark. In 2003 Germany questioned whether its support for the United States still could or even should be unconditional.

The Iraq crisis undercut Germany's historic insistence on avoiding the fundamental choice between Washington and Paris. Berlin's choice in the Iraq crisis was interpreted in Central Europe as pressure to choose the EU over the American option. Here lay the paradox of Germany's position on Iraq: On the one hand, Germany has a vital national interest in fostering a strong and cohesive European Union, especially in light of the inevitable pressures of adjustment to post-2004 enlargement; on the other hand, the decision to separate its Iraq policy from America's position and the concomitant deterioration of German-American relations deepened the fissures within the EU, especially with countries that look to continued U.S. engagement in Europe as an irreducible national security imperative. That applies not just to the postcommunist democracies or some of the small Nordic states. It applies, importantly, to German relations with the United Kingdom because of London's special relationship with Washington on the one hand and London's critical importance to any future viability of the ESDP on the other.

On February 7, 2004, during the 40th Munich Conference on Security Policy, German Foreign Minister Joschka Fischer and Defense Minister Peter Struck articulated their government's position on NATO's future and the relationship between NATO and the ESDP. The views presented by Fischer and Struck were especially significant considering that the 2003 conference was consumed with argument over the decision to go to war in Iraq. Most significant was that Fischer reaffirmed his government's view that the decision not to go to war was correct but at the same time offered to move forward, asserting that now that the war had started, "firstly, the coalition must bring the war to a successful conclusion as quickly as possible, and secondly, the peace must be won."[20]

Fischer's position was that failure in Iraq would have negative consequences for both America and Europe, for both prowar and antiwar countries alike. The position offered an opening to the United States and to the Europeans by sending a message that although Germany continued to oppose the war in principle, it was ready to aid in the reconstruction effort in Iraq. Fischer also took the position that the United Nations ought to play the key role in transferring sovereignty to the Iraqis as quickly as possible. More poignant about his Munich Security Conference speech was Fischer's declaration that Germany would not stand in the way of consensus on a NATO operation in Iraq, even though it would not contribute troops on the ground.

In a rather perplexing twist for a speech delivered by a member of Germany's Green Party, Fischer raised the broader issue of the "modernization crisis" in the Middle East and the region's inability to find "any answers to the pressing challenges of the twenty-first century" or to "meet the expectations of a predominantly young population."[21] Fischer articulated the position that, while it was important whether NATO would engage in Iraq, it was absolutely critical whether the U.S. and Europe could finally effectively address stabilization and modernization issues in the Middle East. Here was the crux of the German approach: calling for a "common strategy" rather than a "toolbox" approach favored by the United States in the coalitions of the willing. Fischer clearly recognized the need for the restoration of an all-out consensus and called for the EU and NATO Mediterranean policy initiatives to be augmented by a new economic partnership to embrace the entire Mediterranean by 2010.

Fischer's vision for new EU/NATO cooperation was amplified by comments delivered by Defense Minister Peter Struck. Struck argued that the "existential crisis of NATO"—a reference to the turmoil over the Article 4 guarantee to Turkey in the run-up to the Iraq war—had passed, but that the question about what future NATO had remained.[22] Struck maintained that although the alliance had taken a decisively global orientation following the 2002 Prague NATO summit, and that it must be able to defend its members' interests wherever they were threatened—as the right strategy for NATO if it were to remain relevant—the creation of the NATO Response Force (NRF) was simply a step to the discussion about the role and operations NATO would undertake under the changed conditions. Using the example of ISAF in Afghanistan, Struck argued that in order for ISAF to succeed, it must remain separate as a stabilization operation from counterterrorist operations. More important, it must be perceived as such. He called for a debate inside NATO about "necessary joint action to be taken in the face of the diverse challenges."[23]

Struck insisted that transatlantic relations must be "renewed and reinforced" but also must be "aligned with the changed conditions and changed partners."[24] The basis for the new transatlantic dialogue, according to Struck, would be the *National Security Strategy of the United States* and the EU's *European Security Strategy*.[25] Struck proposed that a "new Harmel Report" be commissioned to outline the NATO of the future, to be presented at the upcoming Istanbul summit in June 2004. The core of Struck's argument was that "effective joint action would only be possible if the Alliance partners developed a common understanding of the future role of the Alliance." Struck rejected the idea that Germany was seeking to build European "counterweights" to a dominant superpower, but said that rather it was attempting to build an "efficient partnership on equal terms between democratic states which are and will remain dependent on one another to guarantee their security."[26]

Struck echoed Fischer's view that a NATO limited to a "toolbox" role would not be viable. Likewise, he said, the development of a complementary relationship between NATO and the EU was crucial for the future of NATO. In the German view, "NATO will continue to be the first choice for crisis operations with the participation of the European and American Alliance partners. On the other hand, the EU has unique possibilities for combining the use of military and civilian instruments, which is particularly important in the case of 'nation building.'"[27] Finally, military capabilities and the contributions of alliance members would be critical to the continued vitality of NATO, which meant that transformation of NATO as a whole would be contingent on transformation and reform within each member state. For Germany, Struck argued, it meant adjusting the Bundeswehr to fit the probable operations of the future, especially "global conflict prevention, and crisis management, including the fight against international terrorism."

American expectations were critical to the revitalization of NATO, as advocated by Defense Minister Struck. The proposal presented at the 2004 Munich conference by U.S. Sen. Richard Lugar spoke directly to those expectations and included a new role for NATO in combating WMD development in the Middle East; stopping WMD proliferation, taking an active role in fighting terrorist networks; protecting sea and land lines of communication;

launching Afghanistan-type operations based on the NRF; and most important, accepting a formal role in Iraq, becoming "comprehensively involved in the Iraqi democratic transformation."[28] However, Lugar's vision did not match NATO's reality. The subsequent June 2004 NATO summit in Istanbul demonstrated to the United States that those expectations could be met only partway, with arguments over whether NATO should train Iraqi security forces on Iraq's territory indicative of the strains in the transatlantic relationship. Likewise, in Istanbul NATO could only offer two thousand additional troops to increase security for the upcoming Afghan elections.

In the end, Germany's decision to side with France and the other countries opposing America's position on Iraq not only had an inevitable impact on German-American relations but also sent a shockwave across Central Europe and the Baltic littoral, registering especially strongly in Poland. The challenge for Germany in 2005 and beyond would be to devise a security policy acceptable to France and the other countries that opposed the U.S. war in Iraq but also aimed at restoring the transatlantic relationship. At the same time, Germany would have to convince the Americans that further attempts to transform NATO into a "toolbox" for missions without building a larger consensus are bound to further weaken and ultimately undermine the alliance.

The latter task will be difficult to accomplish, especially in light of the comments delivered by Defense Minister Struck on behalf of Chancellor Schröder during the 41st annual security conference in Munich on February 13, 2005, during which the Germans called for replacing NATO with a new formula for U.S. consultations with Europe. Speaking on the chancellor's behalf, Struck asserted that NATO was "no longer the primary venue where transatlantic partners discuss and coordinate strategies," and that "the dialogue between the European Union and the United States . . . in its current form does justice neither to the Union's growing importance nor to the new demands on transatlantic cooperation." Speaking on Schröder's behalf, Struck urged the EU and the United States to set up a panel of independent officials to analyze the current conditions of the relationship and to report not later than in 2006 on the alternatives to the current NATO structures.

As Struck asserted, both sides "should focus with even greater determination and resolve on the task of adapting our cooperation structures to the changed conditions and challenges."[29] Although his Munich speech was criticized by both NATO Secretary General Jaap de Hoop Scheffer and the White House, it suggested that Germany would likely continue to take steps, albeit hesitantly, toward building the European security architecture around the European Union and that Germany was openly declaring for the first time that the European Union ranked higher than NATO in its priorities in the area of national security policy.

THE UNITED STATES AND POLAND SPECIAL PARTNERSHIP

The first post–Cold War decade of Polish foreign policy rested on the assumption that the country needed to bridge between the European Union, especially Germany, and the United States. Always concerned about Moscow's intentions, postcommunist Warsaw has seen NATO membership and the continued U.S. commitment to European security as the ultimate guarantee of its recovered independence. The other leg of Polish security policy has been European Union membership and strong relations with Germany. The two goals were framed by Warsaw's policy imperative to avoid choosing between Europe on the one hand and America on the other. Iraq changed the dynamic, offering Poland the opportunity to choose to build a special relationship with the United States, even at the risk of paying the price in its relationship with Germany, as in fact happened. The damage was done not only in government-to-government relations but also in how Poland was perceived by the German public.

American security relations with Poland are close, although it would be an exaggeration to speak of a "strategic partnership," and Poland's support of American policy in Iraq was rewarded with additional military assistance from Washington. In February 2005 the Bush administration announced that Poland would receive a grant of $100 million from a new U.S. "solidarity initiative," which, according to the U.S. government's statement, has been extended to "assist nations such as Poland, which have taken political and economic risks in order to act on their convictions".[30] The additional assistance came after Poland's defense minister, Jerzy Szmajdziński, confirmed that Poland would sustain its deployment at seventeen hundred troops, plus seven hundred standby reserves, through December 31, 2005. Military aid to Poland would be included in the $81-billion supplemental military spending requested by the Bush administration in 2005. The name given to the U.S. assistance program had unmistakable symbolism, invoking the memory of the Polish Solidarity labor movement of the 1980s. It was perhaps indicative of how limited Poland's influence in Washington still was that the Bush administration's $100-million "solidarity" package to Poland was subsequently dropped by the Congress from the 2005 appropriations, although selected for possible inclusion in the 2006 budget.[31]

Poland's value to the United States became apparent during the so-called "Orange Revolution" in Ukraine in the fall of 2004. During that time, Poland's President Aleksander Kwaśniewski proved to be an important force in bringing about a peaceful resolution of the confrontation and the negotiation of the second round of elections and the transfer of power to Viktor Yushchenko's reform camp. In the course of the crisis, Poland played a central role, with Kwaśniewski working in tandem with EU's Javier Solana during their negotiating mission to Kiev and Secretary of State Colin Powell staying in the background. More important, as a member of the European Union, Poland would offer the United States another important asset in its relationship with Europe, as shown by the pressure Kwaśniewski contributed to the European Commission's proactive stance on Ukrainian elections.[32] The price Poland paid for supporting democracy in Ukraine was further chilling of its relations with Russia.

Although Poland is too weak to be a genuine partner for the Americans, the new relationship between the United States and Poland has been reflected in the frequency of high-level government contacts. Between 2000 and 2005 President Kwaśniewski visited the White House four times, and in addition to the summit meetings, Washington and Warsaw have maintained frequent contacts at the level of foreign and defense ministers. Between 2003 and 2005 there was also an increase in high-level military-to-military discussions, including exchanges of visits between the chairman of the Joint Chiefs and the chief of the Polish General Staff. The United States' close relationship with Poland is part of a larger shift in emphasis to Central Europe. To convey a symbolic message to the "new allies," President George W. Bush chose Bratislava, the capital of Slovakia, for his February 2005 summit meeting with Russia's President Vladimir Putin. The symbolism of the White House actions was augmented by congressional support for Polish military modernization, which increased the annual military assistance to Poland from $12 million to $66 million annually.

One outstanding and irksome problem in U.S.–Polish relations is the continued visa requirement for Polish citizens traveling to the United States—an issue raised repeatedly by the Polish president and the Polish prime minister during their visits to Washington. The compromise offered by the United States to the Poles in 2004 was a "road map" that would streamline visa processing for the Poles and provide for prescreening by U.S. immigration officers at Polish airports to ensure that the Poles who might be denied entry into the United States would be turned back in Poland rather than incur the additional cost of a return trip from the United States.

The United States' policy toward Central Europe, especially Poland, remains tied to American relations with Germany. The effort of the second Bush administration to improve relations with Germany, including the February 2005 visit by Secretary of State Condoleezza Rice and President Bush's summit meeting with Chancellor Schröder, underscored the inherent limitation in America's reliance on the "new" Europeans as its principal partners in the region. Without cooperation from Germany, the United States is likely to encounter continuing difficulties in maintaining the political viability of NATO.

U.S.–EU COUNTERTERRORIST POLICIES AND REGIONAL COOPERATION

Despite continued friction across the Atlantic over the decision to go to war in Iraq, the United States has been able to rely on the European Union, including North and Central Europe, for support in its effort to combat international terrorism. It is perhaps a testimony to the remarkable strength of the residual transatlantic ties that divisions over Iraq did not undermine counterterrorism cooperation in the region and across Europe, especially in light of the fact that the United States accentuated the Continental fault lines on policy in the run-up to the Iraq war. Cooperation with European police and intelligence services has been critical to the success of the American counterterrorism effort, especially because the September 11 attack against the United States originated in Europe.

In contrast to the rift within NATO over Iraq, there is an EU commitment to counterterrorist cooperation with the United States, especially in the area of intelligence and police cooperation. In a gesture symbolic of the rank assigned to cooperation with the United States, the first foreign trip in May 2004 by Gijs De Vries, the new European coordinator for counterterrorism, was made to Washington. Speaking at the Center for Strategic and International Studies, De Vries emphasized three principles of the EU's counterterrorism strategy: that it was a common fight for Europe and the United States, that the EU was fully committed to combating terrorism, and most important, that neither the EU nor the United States could succeed, one without the other. In addition to sharing the view that terrorism is a threat to common values of free and democratic societies, De Vries emphasized the significance of Europe's considerable experience in combating terrorism in the years prior to September 11, as terrorist attacks in Britain, Ireland, and Spain alone had cost more than five thousand European lives.[33]

There is considerable overlap between U.S. and EU counterterrorism strategies, though important differences as well. The American strategy has been focusing on five broad fronts: diplomatic, military, intelligence, law enforcement, and financial.[34] American and European counterterrorist cooperation was strengthened in the aftermath of the March 11, 2004, bombing of commuter trains in Madrid, for it brought to the fore the realization that Europe is just as vulnerable to terrorism as the United States. The Madrid bombing prompted the strengthening of U.S./EU cooperation in combating terrorism, even as it emphasized the split between Europe and the United States over policy in Iraq. The EU created the European Arrest Warrant, which requires all EU police forces to arrest a suspect and to extradite him to the country within the EU that has issued the warrant. The EU created joint investigation teams to permit law enforcement from different EU countries to work together on a joint counterterrorist investigation. It established the nascent Eurojust, a pan-European law enforcement organization that should, once fully developed, strengthen coordination of counterterrorist operations. The EU also adopted legislation that provides for the freezing of assets of persons, groups, or organizations involved in financing and assisting terrorist activities. It includes strengthening laws directed against money laundering through EU banks. The final, and perhaps potentially most effective, step was to give the EU's police agency, the Europol, a broader role in collecting, sharing, and analyzing information about international terrorist groups, as well as the specific provision for Europol participation in joint investigative teams.

At the core of counterterrorist cooperation between the United States and the European Union are two agreements that permit Europol to share intelligence and personnel data with the U.S. Department of Homeland Security and U.S. law enforcement agencies. One area in which cooperation has been critical to U.S. counterterrorism efforts was joint work among the United States, Europol, and Interpol to keep track of lost and stolen passports. In 2003 the United States and the EU concluded an Extradition and Mutual Assistance Agreement to accelerate extradition requests, especially in cases involving terrorism. The agreement also enables the United States to gain access to bank records in Europe, with reciprocity for European investigations. The next step is likely to be the creation of joint U.S.–EU investigative teams working on terrorism investigations. In North and Central Europe, the United States has completed bilateral agreements for cooperation in counterterrorist investigations.

Where the American and European approaches to terrorist threats diverge is in the area of direct application of military power to combating terrorism. The EU approach emphasizes greater coordination in economic assistance to relieve what De Vries termed the "endemic poverty, illiteracy, unemployment, and human misery that foster the resentment in which the support for terrorism can grow."[35] In contrast, while Washington remains committed to economic assistance as a way to deal with deeper causes of terrorism, the United States' policy is much more proactive when it comes to the use of military power to attack terrorist strongholds directly and to eradicate terrorist organizations. The important distinction between the American and European visions of counterterrorism goes to the heart of divergent views between the U.S. and the EU on the efficacy of the use of military power, especially direct military intervention in the Middle East.

Another difference is on how to handle potential threats of Weapons of Mass Destruction. Where the European Union has been emphatic in its insistence that diplomacy must be pushed to the utmost to alleviate the WMD threat, the United States has been considerably less willing to permit diplomacy to work indefinitely. Here American relations with individual North and Central European states have run directly into the problem of differences among the EU members on the efficacy of military power and the relative effectiveness of diplomacy where limiting threats of WMD is concerned. As the fracturing of EU consensus over Iraq has demonstrated, the United States has been able to rely on the new EU members in Central Europe and the Baltic littoral to support its more proactive view of the application of military force to counterterrorism and combating the WMD threat, notwithstanding the price those countries have had to pay for their pro-American stance.

The biggest challenge facing the ongoing efforts to better integrate American and European counterterrorism efforts is the continued fluctuation of linkages between NATO and EU member states. In the Nordic-Baltic region and in Central Europe, the United States remains in a strong position vis-à-vis the EU as a whole, as it continues to be able to leverage the strong pro-American sentiments of the Poles, the Balts, Norway, and Denmark, while it seeks to work closely with Germany, Sweden, and Finland. Most important, the United States' counterterrorism policy and its ability to cooperate with both its principal regional partners and with the EU as a whole are helped by the fact that, in contrast to their lack of agreement on mission in the Middle East, the Europeans and the Americans generally agree on the vital importance of intelligence and police cooperation, transparency of financial records, and diplomatic efforts to the common cause of combating the terrorist threat.

NOTES

1. For a representative example of these debates, see *Defending Europe: The EU, NATO and the Quest for European Autonomy,* ed. Jolyon Howorth and John T. S. Keeler, (New York: Palgrave Macmillan, 2003).

2. Author's interviews with American officers directing various aspects of the Kosovo operation, their views expressed on background.

3. White House, "President Bush Speaks to Faculty and Students of Warsaw University," Warsaw, Poland, June 15, 2001.

4. I am grateful to Chris Donnelly for the insights on the evolution, NATO Headquarters, Brussels, July 2001.

5. Author's interviews with British defense officials, the Ministry of Defense, London, October 2001.

6. Author's interviews with British defense officials.

7. *Proceedings: NATO Enlargement After 2002: Opportunities and Challenges,* Washington, DC: National Defense University, 2001.

8. Author's interview with Lise Rasmussen, Danish Mission, NATO Headquarters, Brussels, October 26, 2001.

9. Author's interviews, NATO Headquarters, Brussels, June 17–18, 2002.

10. "German Town Wary of U.S. Troop Pullout," *New York Times,* August 17, 2004.

11. Howorth and Keeler, 10.

12. Howorth and Keeler, 11.

13. For the Mitchell plan see Sharm el-Sheikh Fact-Finding Committee, *The Mitchell Plan, April 30, 2001, The Avalon Project at Yale Law School,* at www.yale.edu/lawweb/avalon/mideast/mitchell_plan.htm. For the Tenet Plan, see George Tenet, *The Tenet Plan: Israeli-Palestinian Ceasefire and Security Plan, Proposed by CIA Director George Tenet; June 13, 2001, The Avalon Project at Yale Law School,* at www.yale.edu/lawweb/avalon/mideast/mid023.htm.

14. Frédéric Bozo, "The Effect of Kosovo and the Danger of Decoupling," in *Defending Europe: The EU, NATO and the Quest for European Autonomy,* ed. Jolyon Howorth and John T. S. Keeler (New York: Palgrave Macmillan, 2003), 70.

15. Author's interview with Ambassador Michael Durkee, SHAPE, Mons, Belgium, June 17, 2002.

16. Author's background interviews, U.S. Mission, NATO Headquarters, Brussels, June 18, 2002.

17. "The European Union and NATO: A Lull Between the Storms," *The Economist,* September 25, 2003.

18. Doug Bereuter, "11 November Address to the Plenary Sitting by the Hon. Doug Bereuter (United States) President of the NATO Parliamentary Assembly," *NATO Parliamentary Assembly Speeches, 2003,* at www.nato-pa.int/Default.asp?SHORTCUT=428.

19. Detlef Puhl, "Germany and the U.S.—What's Next? Repair the Damage?" *American Institute for Contemporary German Studies,* at www.aicgs.org/c/puhl.shtml.

20. Joschka Fischer, "Speech, the 40th Munich Conference on Security Policy" (translation of advance text, Munich, Germany, February 7, 2004), www.europarl.eu.int/meetdocs/committees/afet/20040217NATO/Fischer.pdf.

21. Fischer, "Speech, the 40th Munich Conference on Security Policy."

22. Peter Struck, "Future of NATO" (speech, 40th Munich Conference on Security Policy, February 7, 2004), www.europarl.eu.int/meetdocs/committees/afet/20040217NATO/Struck.pdf.

23. Struck, "Future of NATO."

24. Struck, "Future of NATO."

25. National Security Council, *The National Security Strategy of the United States of America* (Washington, DC: U.S. Government Printing Office, 2002), www.whitehouse.gov.nsc/nss.pdf; and European Council, *A Secure Europe in a Better World: European Security Strategy* (Brussels: Council of the European Union, December 12, 2003), http://ue.eu.int/uedocs/cmsUpload/78367.pdf.

26. Struck, "Future of NATO."

27. Struck, "Future of NATO."

28. Senator Richard G. Lugar, "NATO and the Greater Middle East" (speech, 40th Munich Conference on International Security, February 7, 2004), www .europarl.eu.int/meetdocs/committees/afet/20040217NATO/Lugar.pdf.

29. Agence France Presse, "Germany Urges NATO Reform and Rethink of Transatlantic Ties" (in English), February 13, 2005.

30. *The Irish Times*, "Pro–U.S. Stance Pays Off for 'New Europe,'" February 12, 2005.

31. Polska Agencja Prasowa PAP, "USA: Pomoc wojskowa dla Polski będzie rozważona w budżecie na 2006 r" [USA: Military assistance to Poland will be considered in the 2006 budget], news release, March 3, 2005.

32. Polska Agencja Prasowa PAP, "Kwaśniewski on Ukrainian Elections," news release, November 8, 2004.

33. Gijs De Vries, "European Strategy in the Fight Against Terrorism and the Cooperation With the United States," (speech at the Center for Strategic and International Studies European Dialogue Lunch, Washington, DC, May 13, 2004).

34. Colin L. Powell, "Opening Remarks," (speech, National Commission on Terrorist Attacks Upon the United States, U.S. Department of State Office of the Spokesman, Washington, DC, March 23, 2004).

35. De Vries.

Conclusion

NORTH AND CENTRAL EUROPE
BETWEEN NATO AND THE EU

*S*ecurity-policy differences among the countries along the EU/NATO northern periphery reflect larger cleavages in Europe as a whole. Although the old Europe–new Europe dichotomy introduced by U.S. Defense Secretary Donald Rumsfeld in the context of the Second Iraq War has not really explained the complex political dynamic on the Continent, we are nevertheless in new territory when it comes to the United States' relations with Europe. Even more important, intra-European relations today are marked by divisions that defy the dream of a "Europe whole and free," which only a few years ago was the mantra of postcommunist transitions. The new transatlantic security dynamic is rooted in different interests and strategic approaches to the security of America and Europe. In North and Central Europe the diversity of approaches to security also draws on different regional geostrategic considerations and different historical legacies.

Perhaps the most striking aspect of security strategy in the 1990s was the continuation of the North Atlantic Treaty Organization as the declared premier security organization of both the United States and Europe. During that period the alliance tried several times to reinvent itself in both political and military terms. Overall, it succeeded admirably in the political arena, going through two cycles of enlargement, in 1999 and 2004, while in the process extending stability and promoting democracy and Western norms of civil-military relations to postcommunist democracies. In the military arena, however, the 1990s were a time of consistent failure to modernize and adapt the allied capabilities and mission to the new challenges facing the transatlantic community. Though NATO went out of area in the Balkans—against Serbia in 1999 over its repression of Albanians in Kosovo—it never managed to establish the same sense of consensus on the nature of the new international security environment that bound the allies during the Cold War.

The ultimate test of the "new" NATO came on September 11, 2001, when the United States, the core member of the alliance, came under attack by al Qaeda and found itself at war with Islamist terrorists. The aftermath of September 11 witnessed two historic firsts: the invocation of Article 5 of the Washington Treaty by the allies in defense of the United States, followed by the decision by the U.S. government to pursue the war in Afghanistan against al Qaeda and the Taliban without relying on alliance structures. Those two events constituted the test of NATO's ability to reconnect its aggregative and structuring functions. In Afghanistan the United States opted to act unilaterally in the military arena, thereby relegating NATO's utility to the structuring function alone. In 2003, with the Second Iraq War, even the structuring function proved no longer operable, setting the military aggregative function of the alliance aside.

Hindsight reveals that the terrorist attacks on the World Trade Center and the Pentagon in 2001 were a watershed for NATO. Throughout the post–Cold War decade NATO was looking for a mission that would justify its continued existence and unite its members in a renewed sense of purpose. On September 11 the mission found NATO: the shared struggle against a common threat of jihadi terrorism that could and should have become NATO's new mission. But that did not happen, despite the expressions of universal solidarity with the United States and limited assistance offered by NATO in both Afghanistan and Iraq. By the time the George W. Bush administration decided to launch a preemptive war against Iraq, the alliance was in freefall, torn by internal dissension, the transatlantic rift between the United States and France and Germany, and the "old" versus "new" Europe cleavage between those who opposed America's policy on Iraq and those who were willing to follow its lead. The difficulties of the postwar occupation of Iraq, the drain it imposed on U.S. forces, and NATO's continued inability to play a meaningful role there have marked the low point for the alliance.

Iraq continues to divide the allies, notwithstanding their other efforts to cooperate; for example, since August 2003 NATO has been in charge of the International Security Assistance Force (ISAF) in Afghanistan. While Afghanistan began the process of NATO's marginalization as a premier military security organization, Iraq pushed it further down that path than anyone could have anticipated only a few years ago. Although the administrative structure of NATO persists and will soldier on into the future, after Iraq the United States and the European Union may have no choice but to look for alternatives. That is nowhere more visible than along Europe's de facto eastern periphery: in North and Central Europe and the Baltic littoral, where the burden of history and continued uncertainty about the future of Russia and its near abroad cast a long shadow.

As NATO has weakened, the United States' policy toward the region has begun to play a defining role. Since the collapse of the Soviet empire, no state has had greater influence on the security architecture in Central Europe and the Baltic region than the United States. Beginning with the Partnership for Peace program in the early 1990s, through the 1997 Madrid decision to invite Poland, Hungary, and the Czech Republic to join the alliance, through the 2002 Prague decision on the second round of post–Cold War enlargement, to the U.S.–led "coalition of the willing" in Iraq, American policy has defined the direction of regional change. In addition, an important trend has resulted from the decomposition of NATO's military capabilities and the widening cracks in U.S.–European relations: the propensity to seek alternatives to NATO either in the European Union's ESDP or, as has been the case especially among post-communist democracies, in close bilateral relations with the United States to offset the atrophy of NATO's military capabilities and the EU's continued weakness in the area of security policy. That tendency is reinforced by the larger context of the dominant American military position in the world, with the added factor of a technological gap between the U.S. armed forces and the armed forces of even the most advanced European allies. In the final analysis, it makes United States policy toward the region and Europe in general the critical determinant of the security architecture in North and Central Europe. And these choices do translate neatly into either a renewed commitment to NATO or the support for the EU to the exclusion of NATO.

This book has sought to gauge the security policy options available to small and medium-size regional powers in post–Cold War Europe as they come to terms with the unraveling transatlantic security system. Its case studies were countries of northern and central Europe because of the benign security environment in which they have operated since 1991. Their security policies show that the structuring function of alliances cannot in fact suffice to sustain NATO, while the future of the ESDP remains in question. The current set of security options in North and Central Europe is not a matter of simply substituting one organization for the other, for even if historical determinants and geostrategic constraints could be set aside, the extent to which NATO and the EU overlap in the region makes such a clean solution difficult to envision. The growing differentiation and polarization among its members is the inherent limitation on the European Union's security project.

Europe is dividing not because the United States has tried to make such divisions into its policy tool (although Washington did exploit intra-European differences during the run-up to the Iraq war), but because these differences are real. They reflect the diversity of interests among states in the European

Union and conflicting priorities among the 15 old members and the 10 new entrants. Since 2004 intra-European differences have been amplified by the very scope of the challenge that the enlarged European Union has posed for the bureaucracy in Brussels. If the countries of north and central Europe differ from Europe's major continental powers, it is not only because it consists of smaller and weaker states, but also because its proximity to Russia adds an important variable that drives the region's security policies. In North and Central Europe the structuring function of both NATO and the EU is always taken in the context of these countries' most rudimentary defense capabilities. As this book has sought to show, northern and central Europeans are keenly aware of their greater vulnerability, and they will continue to measure the value of NATO and the ESDP in that light. Depending on their history and their geostrategic position, some states in the region emphasize the traditional defensive function of NATO; others opt for the emerging ESDP; yet others seek to strengthen their ties with the United States.

North and Central Europe constitutes a microcosm of the larger problems confronting European and transatlantic security. These countries' often divergent views on the relative value of NATO and the ESDP underscore the fact that those organizations are in transition. The region's security identity is in flux, with historically determined preferences for alignment or the lack thereof. Today the Nordic balancing of the Cold War era has shifted significantly toward a larger European security identity, but the process has been uneven, with greater adaptation in Finland and Sweden as against the continued preference for the transatlantic NATO link in Denmark and Norway. The three new Baltic democracies—Estonia, Latvia, and Lithuania—look to the United States as the ultimate guarantor of their security, even though since 2004 they have all been members of the European Union. Germany and Poland remain at the center of the ongoing security identity transformation, with Germany becoming ever more the core of the emerging ESDP and Poland playing a high-stakes game to become America's closest partner within the EU, the quintessential "new" ally.

The declining military utility of the NATO alliance has had a significant impact on the security calculus of the Central European–Baltic/Nordic region. The region is the bellwether of how security policy is likely to be conceptualized in Europe in the coming decade. Assuming that the process of NATO's decomposition continues, the states in the region are left with the overriding priority either to strengthen their transatlantic connection to the United States or to focus their security policies on the European Union's ESDP. It also forces those that are EU members to choose the role they will play in the enlarged European Union. The choice between NATO, the EU, or bilateralism may never be truly complete, offering concerned states some combination of all three alternatives as the foundation of security policies in the region.

To the countries of northern and central Europe, as a frontier of the enlarged European Union and NATO, traditional hard security concerns remain more important than they do among the countries farther west. Not only is the region more exposed to threats from Russia and its near abroad, but it also has historically justified reasons to remain concerned about the direction of political change in the Russian Federation. Hence the key variable for North and Central European security is Russia's future. Regardless of how the U.S.–EU relationship ultimately evolves, Russia's ambition to be a player in Central Europe is likely to persist, possibly set against its competition with America and Europe for influence in Ukraine, the Caucasus, and Central Asia. For the states in North and Central Europe, their peripheral status and the continued uncertainty about Russia's political evolution underscore the traditional security dimension of their policy choices.

Finally, changes in North and Central European security are the result not only of the weakness of NATO as a military security organization but also of the ongoing transformation of the region. The dual enlargement of NATO and the EU in 2004 can be viewed as the closing of doors on the Cold War legacy in Central Europe: The region has set aside the moniker "postcommunist," and while a number of problems rooted in the four decades of communist control remain, the issues it confronts are largely those of new democracies at different levels of consolidation. It is also reasonable to assume that in the coming decade the European Union will become an ever more significant influence in the region, for in contrast to NATO membership, being a member of the European Union is an ever-present factor in all areas of economics and politics and, with the evolution of the ESDP, also increasingly in the area of national security.

That leaves the key question about the impact of the second post–Cold War round of NATO enlargement on Central Europe and the Baltic region, for both the 1999 and 2004 entrants have looked to NATO to solve their historical insecurity dilemmas, including their residual concerns about Russia. In the months after its 2003 Iraq operation started going badly for the United States, there was growing concern about NATO's ability to provide for the security of the region. Notwithstanding their official optimism, governments in Warsaw, Vilnius, and Riga grew worried that NATO was in trouble as a military alliance, perhaps heading for the history books faster than many a politician seemed able to admit.

ALLIANCE OR ALIGNMENT?

Historically, alliances have been *against* something or someone, and only derivatively *for* something. During the Cold War, NATO's core function was to defend Europe against Soviet aggression, while other tasks, such as fostering a community of shared democratic values or enlarging the area of stability, were secondary. It was the scope of the external threat that ultimately made the alliance manageable during the Cold War, for regardless of policy differences among its members NATO's core business served as the foundation of allied consensus.

The two cycles of enlargement with the attendant conditionality have completed NATO's transformation into first and foremost a political organization. In its post–Cold War reformulation, NATO's order of priorities has been reversed. Today the alliance knows what it is *for* without first having decided what it is *against*. The consequence of that has been the hollowing-out of the alliance, first in terms of its military capabilities and more recently in terms of its political manageability. Even though its members are bound by the residual institutional structure, NATO today represents less a cohesive alliance than a looser political alignment of states. For example, in the era of global terrorism, NATO has thus far been unable to define its core mission in a way that would sustain political decision making. Although the terrorist threat is real, however, it is not shared equally or defined the same way by all. To the degree NATO lacks the foundation of a shared mission, its political mechanism has become dysfunctional. NATO's commitment to shared values and institutions, rather than common defense, is increasingly the principal reason for its continued existence.

In consequence, transatlanticism in the form that had once defined U.S.–European relations clearly belongs to the past. Perhaps NATO's devolution from a collective defense organization into a collective security organization was inevitable once the principal threat to Europe's security had been eliminated, as it took away from Europe the imperative to follow America's lead and to pool national resources for defense. The mixed record of the 1999 enlargement, NATO's ambivalent response to September 11, internal fracturing over the 2003 Iraq war, and the politics of dual enlargement have defined the limits of the new NATO. While NATO struggles to formulate its new mission, the Europeans are exploring the viability of the ESDP, bilateral relations with the United States, and regional security cooperation. It has been a Europe-wide phenomenon; likewise, as this book has argued, in North and Central Europe NATO is competing for influence with the European Union and the United States, inasmuch as support for or opposition to American policy defines the security policies of the states in the region. As of 2005 NATO could still play a role in transatlantic relations and, to a lesser extent, in relations among its European members, but its structuring function alone may not be enough to hold Europe and America together in the future.

Although the hollowing-out of NATO does not necessarily mean that the alliance is doomed, it does raise a question about its long-term viability as a military security organization. For North and Central European states, especially new postcommunist democracies, the answer to this question is key to their current and future security position in the region. The coming decade will determine whether the alliance can still rebuild itself as the focus of transatlantic relations or will become militarily less relevant. The internal crisis over NATO's guarantees to Turkey under Article 4 on the eve of the 2003 Iraq war and the subsequent polarization within NATO showed that even extreme outcomes are not out of the question. The range of negative scenarios includes increased competition between the European Union and the United States; the complete irrelevance of NATO within the next ten to twenty years, accompanied by the emergence of a working and active ESDP but possibly comprising fewer than the present twenty-five EU members; or even an all-out fracturing within the European Union over security policy, followed by a breakup and a complete preference of some Europeans for American leadership coupled with increased tension across the Atlantic. All of these extreme outcomes would leave both the United States and Europe worse off, and they would be especially damaging to the security of North and Central Europe and the Baltic littoral.

Even with continued American leadership, the experience of the 2004 and 2005 strongly suggests that, regardless of the skepticism about NATO's future exhibited by Germany's Schröder government or the continued enthusiasm for NATO and American leadership in the alliance demonstrated by the Poles, the Balts, the Danes, and the Norwegians, NATO may prove less and less able to function as a framework for dialogue between Europe and America. While the question about the ultimate capability of NATO to keep the security of the United States and Europe interconnected is yet to be answered, the 2003 crisis over Iraq showed that NATO in and of itself was not enough to enable Europe to reach a consensus on policy.

From the U.S. point of view, the continued paucity of usable military capabilities is more than any other factor at the heart of NATO's present crisis. The alliance is already stretched in its limited operation in Afghanistan, facing continued challenges following the September 2004 elections there. It has shown no desire to commit military forces to help shore up the U.S. forces in Iraq, even though it did provide support for the deployment of the Polish-led international division. For the United States the problem of NATO's declining relevance lies in the declining utility of the alliance in confronting the most intense security threats in the world, especially terrorism and WMD proliferation. Simply put, since September 11, 2001, the U.S. has regarded the dearth of European NATO forces available for out-of-area operations and perhaps even more the absence of political will in key European capitals to deploy meaningful military resources outside of Europe as indicators of NATO's malaise. As this book has argued, the decision to bring seven new

members into the alliance in 2004, all of which had serious capabilities problems, was a signal that in the military sense Washington considers NATO's
value to be marginal. While NATO's emphasis on collective and cooperative
security, which emerged in the 1990s, has been the foundation of its continued relevance in Europe, it is insufficient from the U.S. vantage point to deal
with global threats. America seeks to engage terrorist threats in the Middle
East, in Central Asia, and elsewhere around the globe, and those are the areas where NATO should matter. It does not, overall, and even where it does,
its role is secondary, as in Afghanistan or in support of the Polish-led division
in Iraq.

The blame for NATO's decline is not limited to Europe; part of it should
be assigned to Washington. For a large number of the European NATO allies, especially Germany and France, the fundamental differences with the
United States over the root causes and solutions to the terrorist threat result
in the implicit rejection of the "cherry-picking" formula applied by Washington to NATO's operations since September 11. Indeed, the goal of maintaining alliance cohesion is directly at odds with the coalition-of-the-willing formula employed by the George W. Bush Administration. While it is true that
Europe is more about diversity than uniformity and that "Europe" as a concept is less a reality than a shorthand applied in American policy discussions,
Washington's propensity to pick coalitions from within NATO on a case-by-
case basis has nonetheless hobbled the already weakening alliance. It pushed
NATO in a direction where differences over policy, such as in Iraq, not only
continue to strain the transatlantic link but also further polarize Europe. As
the deadlock in NATO over Turkey in the run-up to the Iraq war demonstrated, the policy differences among the European NATO allies have come
dangerously close to negating the very foundations of their collective defense.
After the 2002 Prague and 2004 Istanbul NATO summits, the United States
and Europe came closer to reaching consensus on the intensity of the terrorist threat, but there is still no agreement on how best to deal with it. Likewise,
the United States and most of the Europeans are poles apart on how to deal
with the Israeli-Palestinian question and on whether U.S.–led regime change
in the Middle East is the right policy. The course of the Iraq war in particular has exposed deep fissures across the Atlantic that, unless a compromise on
Middle East policy is reached, will further hollow out the transatlantic alliance.

The end of the Cold War and more than a decade of democratization
and market reform remade the political landscape in Europe. The 1990s
seemed to have prefigured a new era of European cooperation framed within
a larger context of transatlantic security cooperation with the United States.
Notwithstanding the myriad problems associated with postcommunist tran-

sition, the decade was one of optimism generated by the end of the Cold War. The Balkan wars showed that the combination of ethnic hatreds, weak state institutions, and populist political manipulation could still lead to war in Europe, but NATO's intervention, including the 1999 war against Serbia and NATO's involvement in the subsequent stabilization operations, seemed to prove that the alliance remained viable and had the capacity to remake itself for the post–Cold War era. It was going to be a new alliance, based on newly defined conditionality and honed for out-of-area operations, but that was seen in Brussels and Washington as proof that the old institutions need not disintegrate or fade away. Indeed, the 1990s witnessed the setting of new norms and institutions that led to the 1999 round of NATO enlargement and laid the foundations for the EU enlargement negotiations, the decision in 2002 to initiate the second round of NATO enlargement, and ultimately the dual EU/NATO enlargement of 2004.

The dual enlargement that was expected to celebrate the final end to Europe's old divisions, however, was overshadowed by bubbling-over of simmering intra-European and transatlantic tensions. On the face of things, the two grand bureaucracies have expanded to embrace the postcommunist region and continued to speak of including Romania and Bulgaria in EU membership in 2007. There is also renewed interest in bringing Turkey into the European Union. The NATO-Russia Council, created in May 2002 to provide a vehicle for closer cooperation between NATO and Russia seemed to have addressed the areas of potential friction on the eastern periphery of the alliance, while the June 2004 NATO summit in Istanbul recommitted the members to the Mediterranean Dialogue, the enhanced Partnership for Peace program, and the continued transformation of the alliance structure. The summit reaffirmed the allies' determination to cooperate in the Global War on Terrorism (GWOT) and to strengthen NATO's operation in Afghanistan.

Notwithstanding the official appearance of unity in 2004 at the Istanbul summit and afterward, several problems came into view that pointed clearly to NATO's new limits. First, though NATO agreed in Istanbul to offer support and training for the new Iraqi forces, it did not deliver on the key American objective of getting NATO troops into Iraq, for France and Germany made any such decision de facto contingent on a UN Security Council resolution. Second, NATO's additional support for the ISAF of some sixty-five hundred troops would be limited to approximately two thousand troops, barely enhancing ISAF's ability to operate effectively outside Kabul, especially as the added force was deployed in two areas: one battalion on the north side of the Hindu Kush mountain range and the other to the south and its immediate vicinity. In consequence of those two decisions, NATO in 2004 faced the possibility of a dual strategic failure, one in Iraq and the other in Afghanistan.

The larger question that this book has sought to address is whether in fact historically peripheral states—in eastern Central Europe, Scandinavia, or the Baltic littoral—can escape the dilemma of choosing alignment even if the policy falls short of membership in an established alliance. It is perhaps not surprising that the age-old question about the national interest of states should reenter with such force into the discussion of the regional security configuration. The diplomatic debacle in the 2003 run-up to the Iraq war brought those very issues into clear relief: notwithstanding the norms and the structures offered by such established security institutions as NATO or such political/economic institutions as the European Union, the countries of North and Central Europe have chosen to come closer to Europe or the United States based on their definitions of national interest, their geostrategic location, and their history. In choosing alignment with the United States or by opting for the Continental/EU orientation, the medium and small powers from the region acted in ways that lent themselves more easily to an analysis grounded in realism than in liberal or constructivist theories. In Central Europe and the Baltic littoral in particular, the general propensity toward bandwagoning with the United States, exhibited not only by the postcommunist states but also by such old NATO members as Denmark, has remained strong. For small states in Europe, especially those in historically insecure geostrategic locations, the tendency to align with the United States is likely to continue, despite the risk of damaging the states' relations with Europe.

By mid-2005 the limitations of NATO and the continuing weakness of the ESDP had caused some countries in North and Central Europe, such as Poland, the Baltic States, and to some extent Denmark and Norway to choose a new type of transatlanticism based on direct ties with the United States. Others, like Finland and Sweden, responded to the decline of NATO by rejecting membership and looking instead to the European Union in combination with their own intrinsic defense capabilities and multilateral international institutions to provide for their national security. For Germany, the most important power in the region and the core state of the European Union, the devolution of NATO and the enlargement of the EU posed the fundamental question about its leadership role on the Continent and its changing relationship with the United States.

The two cycles of enlargement, the experience of the Balkan wars, and the inability to respond effectively to September 11 have remade the NATO alliance to the extent that it has lost much of its former character: a war-fighting, collective-defense organization. Paradoxically, as an increasingly political vehicle for multilateral security consultations, NATO today seems to be turning into what the EU's security dimension once was, i.e., a forum where policies and standards were discussed and harmonized but where little action could be taken. NATO's limitations as an alliance have also had an impact on the European Union itself. The transformation of NATO from a collective-defense organization into a collective-security organization has deemphasized NATO's traditional military function, thereby blurring the once clear distinction between the two organizations. Repeated attempts to restore NATO's shared sense of mission to serve as the glue holding Europe and America together, witnessed for instance at the 2004 Istanbul summit, have thus far failed. At twenty-six members and with more applicants waiting in line to join, NATO has morphed from an alliance into an organization having as its foremost purpose continuing to enlarge, so as to keep the concept of an open security community alive. Unless NATO's aggregative function is restored, such an alliance will no longer have the strength to sustain an effective defense community, making realignment within the European Union and across the Atlantic based on the national interests of individual states almost inevitable.

Bibliography

Adler, Emanuel, and Michael Barnett, eds. *Security Communities*. Cambridge: Cambridge University Press, 1998.

Agence France Presse. "Germany Urges NATO Reform and Rethink of Transatlantic Ties." News release, February 13, 2005.

———. "NATO to Test Rapid Reaction Force in Scotland Naval Exercise," News release, September 11, 2003.

———. "US Senate Passes 447 Billion Dollar Defense Budget for Fiscal 2005." News release, July 24, 2004.

Aldis, Anne C., and Roger N. McDermott, eds. *Russian Military Reform, 1992–2002*. Portland, OR: Frank Cass Publishers, 2003.

Allin, Dana H., and Steven Simon. "America's Predicament." *Survival* 46, no. 4 (November 2004): 7–30.

Ames, Paul. "Terror Fight Transforms NATO, Chief Says." *Associated Press Online*, April 1, 2003.

Andréani, Gilles, Christoph Bertram, and Charles Grant. *Europe's Military Revolution*. London: Centre for European Reform, 2001.

———. "The 'War on Terror': Good Cause; Wrong Concept." *Survival* 46, no. 4 (November 2004): 31–50.

Assembly of WEU. *The EU Headline Goal and the NATO Response Force (NRF)—Reply to the Annual Report of the Council*. Document A/1825. Paris, France: Interparliamentary European Security and Defence Assembly, 2003. www.assemblyweu .org/en/documents/sessions_ordinaires/rpt/2003/1825.html.

Associated Press Worldstream. "Belgium Seeks Leaner Forces in Military Overhaul." December 3, 2003.

———. "NATO's Rapid Reaction Force to Be Up and Running Before 2004, Top Alliance General Says." News release, December 4, 2002.

Association of International Experts on the Development of the Kaliningrad Region. *EU-Russia Partnership on Kaliningrad*. Moscow: MEMO2/02/169, July 12, 2002. http://kaliningradexpert.org/stuff/docs/EU-Russia Partnership on Kaliningrad_eng .doc.

Auswärtiges Amt. "Relations Between Australia and Germany." April 2004. www.auswaertiges-amt.de/www/en/laenderinfos/laender/laender_ausgabe _html?type_id=14&land_id=13.

Azizian, Rouben. "A Marriage of Convenience: Russia's Response to U. S. Security Policies." In Stackpole, *Asia-Pacific Responses to U. S. Security Policies,* 1–9. Honolulu: Asia Pacific Center for Security Studies, 2003.

Baker, James A. "Russia in NATO?" *The Washington Quarterly* 25, no. 1 (Winter 2002): 95–103.

Barrie, Douglas. "Britain Determines Military Net Value." *Aviation Week & Space Technology* 157, no. 26 (December 23, 2002): 53–55.

Barry, Charles L. "Transforming NATO Command and Control for Future Missions." *Defense Horizons* 28 (June 2003): 1–11.

"Basic Facts on the Estonian Defence Forces." *NATO's Nations and Partners for Peace* (2001): 8–11.

Baymuratov, M. A., and A. A. Delinskiy. *Mezhdunarodno-pravovyye aspekty stanovleniya i razvitiya evropeyskoy sistemy bezopasnosti na poroge XXI veka.* Odessa: Yuridichnaya literatura, 2004.

Becher, Klaus. "German Forces in International Military Operations," *Orbis* 48, no. 3 (Summer 2004): 397–408.

"Belgium." *Military Technology* 28, no. 1 (January 2004): 81–83.

Belkin, Alexander A. "US-Russian Relations and the Global Counter-Terrorist Campaign." *Journal of Slavic Military Studies.* 17, no. 1 (March 2004): 13–28.

Bereuter, Doug. "11 November Address to the Plenary Sitting by the Hon. Doug Bereuter (United States) President of the NATO Parliamentary Assembly." *NATO Parliamentary Assembly Speeches, 2003.* www.nato-pa.int/Default.asp?SHORTCUT =428.

"Between Two Worlds: Mainland Russia, Kaliningrad and the EU." *Economist.* June 27, 2002.

Binnendijk, Hans and Richard Kugler. "Transforming European Forces." *Survival* 44, no. 3 (Autumn 2002): 117–32.

Blank, Stephen. "Russia and the Baltics in the Age of NATO Enlargement." *Parameters* 28, no. 3 (Autumn 1998): 50–68.

———. "Russia, NATO Enlargement, and the Baltic States." *World Affairs* 160, no. 3 (Winter 1998): 115–125.

Bogdan, Corneliu, and Eugen Preda. *Spheres of Influence.* Boulder, CO: Social Science Monographs; New York: Distributed by Columbia University Press, 1988.

Book, Elizabeth G. "Budget Surge Marks Shift in Dutch Defense." *National Defense* 87, no. 588 (November 2002): 12–13. www.nationaldefensemagazine.org/issues/ 2002/Nov/Budget_Surge.htm.

Bozo, Frédéric. "The Effect of Kosovo and the Danger of Decoupling." In *Defending Europe: The EU, NATO and the Quest for European Autonomy,* edited by Jolyon Howorth and John T. S. Keeler, 61–77. New York: Palgrave Macmillan, 2003.

British Broadcasting Corporation. "Danish Centre-Right Win New Term." *BBC News,* February 8, 2005. http://news.bbc.co.uk/1/hi/world/europe/4245239.stm.

Brovkin, Vladmir. "Who Is With Whom: The United States, the European Union, and Russia on the Eve of War in Iraq." *Demokratizatsiya* 11, no. 2 (Spring 2003): 212. www.findarticles.com/p/articles/mi_qa3996/is_200304/ai_n9199156.

Brzezinski, Zbigniew, and F. Stephen Larrabee. *U. S. Policy toward Northeastern Europe, Report of an Independent Task Force.* Council on Foreign Relations Press, 1999.

Burns, R. Nicholas. "NATO and the Greater Middle East." United States Mission to NATO. May 18, 2004. nato.usmission.gov/ambassador/2004/20040518_Brussels .htm.

Burns, Robert. "Allied Leaders Face Mock Crisis to Spur 'Creative Thinking' About Rapid-Reaction Force." *The Associated Press State & Local Wire*, October 8, 2003.

Bush, George W. "Joint Statement Between the United States of America and the Russian Federation." *Weekly Compilation of Presidential Documents* 39, 40 (October 6, 2003): 1279.

Cagaptay, Soner. "NATO's Transformative Powers." *National Review Online* (April 2, 2004).

Campbell, Kurt M. "The End of Alliances? Not So Fast." *Washington Quarterly* 27, 2 (Spring 2004): 151–63.

"Can Russia Handle a Changed World?" *Economist* 360, no. 8237 (September 1, 2001): 9.

Carlsen, Per. "From the Baltic States to the Caucasus: Regional Co-operation After the Enlargements." *Lithuanian Policy Review* 9, (2002).

Caryl, Christian. "Trouble Next Door; As the EU Pushes East, It Will Run Up Against a Very Messy Backyard." *Newsweek International Edition* (August 12, 2002): 16.

Chamberlin, Jefffrey. "Comparisons of U. S. and Foreign Military Spending: Data from Selected Public Sources." *Congressional Research Service Report for Congress*, January 28, 2004.

Chiu, Daniel Y. "International Alliances in the Power Cycle Theory of State Behavior." *International Political Science Review: ISPR* 24, no. 1 (January 2003): 123–36.

Choroszy, Ryszard. "Dywidenda od wojny." *Polska Zbrojna – Artykuł.* www .polskazbrojina.pl/drukuj.html?id_artykul=1163.

Christensen, Svend Aage. "The Danish Experience. Denmark in NATO 1949–1999." In *Small States and Alliances*, 89–100, ed. Erich Reiter and Heinz Gärtner, Heidelberg and New York: Physica-Verlag, 2001.

Christensen, Thomas, and Jack Snyder. "Chain Gangs and Passed Bucks: Predicting Alliance Patterns in Multipolarity." *International Organization* 44 (Spring 1990): 137–68.

CNN.com, "EU, Russia Deal on Kaliningrad," November 11, 2002.

Cohen, Ariel. "Strategic Cooperation Key to U. S.-Russia Summit." *The Heritage Foundation.* November 15, 2002. www.heritage.org/Research/RussiaandEurasia/ EM839.cfm.

Colston, John. "Military Matters: Marrying Capabilities to Commitments." *NATO Review* (Summer 2004).

Cornish, Paul. "NRF: NATO Response Force or NATO's Rediscovered Future?" London: King's College, July 7, 2003.

Council on Foreign Relations. "Iraq: The War's Price Tag." News release, June 7, 2004. www.cfr.org.

"The Czech Republic." *Military Technology* 28, no. 1 (January 2004): 92–94.

Dąbrowski, Tomasz. *Polska i Niemcy w rozszerzonej Unii Europejskiej—nowe koalicje, nowe rozwiązania.* Warszawa: Centrum Stosunków Miądzynarodowych, July 2003.

Danish Defence. *The Danish Defense Agreement 2005–2009.* Copenhagen: Defense Command Denmark. http://forsvaret. dk/FKO/eng/Defence+Agreement/default.htm?Mode=Print&Site=fko.

"Dark Skies to the East: Russia and the European Union." *Economist.* February 19, 2004: 38.

"Denmark." *Military Technology* 28, no. 1 (January 2004): 94–96.

David, Charles-Philippe, and Jacques Lévesque, eds. *The Future of NATO: Enlargement, Russia, and European Security.* Montreal: McGill-Queen's University Press, 1999.

Davies, Norman. *Rising '44: The Battle for Warsaw.* London: Viking Penguin, 2004.

"Dążenia Litwy, Łotwy i Estonii do integracji z NATO i UE a stosunki tych krajów z Rosją." Warsaw: Ośrodek Studiów Wschodnich, January 2003.

"Declaration on Combating Terrorism." Brussels, March 25, 2004. www.statewatch.org/news/2004/mar/eu-terr-decl.pdf.

"The Defence Industry in Sweden." *NATO's Nations and Partners for Peace* 49, no. 1 (2004): 174–76.

De Vries, Gijs. "European Strategy in the Fight Against Terrorism and the Cooperation with the United States." Speech, CSIS European Dialogue Lunch, Washington, DC, May 13, 2004.

Deighton, Anne. "The European Security and Defense Policy." *Journal of Common Market Studies.* 40, no. 4 (November 2002): 719–41.

Deitchman, S. J. "Military Force Transformation: Progress, Costs, Benefits and Task Remaining." Washington DC: The Atlantic Council of the United States, Occasional Paper, December 2004.

Donnelly, Chris. "Building a NATO Partnership for the Greater Middle East." *NATO Review* (Spring 2004).

Dörfer, Ingemar. *The Nordic Nations in the New Western Secrity Regime.* Washington, DC: Woodrow Wilson Center Press, 1997.

Dragsdahl, Jorgen. "NATO Resists Pressures to Militarise Central Europe." *Basic Papers* 28 (July 1998).

Eke, Stephen. "Russia Eyes New EU With Concern." *BBC News.* April 26, 2004.

Erbe, Jürgen. "Germany Approves A400M Airlifter Purchase." *Jane's Defense Weekly,* May 28, 2003.

Erbe, Jürgen, and Andrew Koch. "Germany Will Streamline Forces to Boost Readiness." *Jane's Defence Weekly,* January 23, 2004.

Eriksson, Johan. "Sweden's Commitment Problem." *Foreign Policy* 137 (July/August 2003): 112.

"Estonia." *Military Technology* 27, no. 1 (January 2003): 92–95.

"Estonian Defence Forces 2003–2006." Tallinn: Estonian Ministry of Defence.

Estonian Ministry of Foreign Affairs. "Baltic Defence Co-operation." Tallinn: Estonian Ministry of Defence, 2002. www.vm.ee/eng/nato/kat_361.

European Council. *A Secure Europe in a Better World: European Security Strategy.* Brussels: Council of the European Union, December 12, 2003. http://ue.eu.int/uedocs/cmsUpload/78367.pdf.

European Parliament. "Lisbon European Council 23 and 24 March 2000, Presidency Conclusions." Luxembourg: European Parliament, 2000. www.europarl.eu.int/summits/lis1_en.htm.

European Security.net. "Rapid Reaction Forces." www.europeansecurity.net/esdpfaqs.html.

"EU-Russia Cooperation Programme/TACIS Russia." *The European Commission's Delegation to Russia,* n.d. www.delrus.cec.eu.int/en/p_260.htm.

Ewens, Michael. "Casualties in Iraq, The Human Cost of Occupation." www.antiwar.com/casualties.

Fairlie, Lyndelle D., and Alexander Sergounin. *Are Borders Barriers? EU Enlargement and the Russian Region of Kaliningrad.* Helsinki and Berlin: Ulkopoliittinen instituutti & Institut fur Europaische Politik, 2001.

"Finland." *Military Technology* 28, no. 1 (January 2004): 94–97.

Fiorenza, Nick. "A Greater Role in the Greater Middle East?" *NATO Notes* 6, no. 1 (February 2004).

Fischer, Joschka. "Speech by Joschka Fischer, Federal Minister for Foreign Affairs, at the 40th Munich Conference on Security Policy." Translation of advance text, Munich, Germany, February 7, 2004. www.europarl.eu.int/meetdocs/committees/afet/20040217NATO/Fischer.pdf.

Frankfurter Allgemeine Zeitung, November 4, 2004.

Frankfurter Allgemeine Zeitung, October 1, 2004.

Friis, Lykke, and Anna Jarosz-Friis. "Countdown to Copenhagen, Big Bang or Fizzle in the EU's Enlargement Process?" Copenhagen: Danish Institute of International Affairs, 2002.

Gangale, Thomas. "Alliance Theory: Balancing, Bandwagoning, and Détente." OPS-Alaska and San Francisco State University, 2003.

Gardner, Hall. "Aligning for the Future." *Harvard International Review.* 24, no. 4 (Winter 2003): 56–61.

Gardner, Hall, ed. *NATO and the European Union: New World, New Europe, New Threats.* Aldershot, UK: Ashgate Publishing Limited, 2004.

George C. Marshall European Center for Security Studies. "Dual Enlargement and the Baltic States: Security Policy Implications." Report of the George C. Marshall Center for Security Studies Conference, Tallinn, Estonia, February 11–13, 2004.

"Germany." *Military Technology* 28, no. 1 (January 2004): 110–18.

Gladkyy, Oleksandr. "American Foreign Policy and U. S. Relations with Russia and China after 11 September." *World Affairs* 166, no. 1 (Summer 2003): 3.

GlobalSecurity.org. "Kaliningrad Special Defense District (KOOR)." GlobalSecurity.org, March 8, 2004. www.globalsecurity.org/military/world/russia/kor-kaliningrad.htm.

Gnesotto, Nicole. "ESDP: The Way Forward." *Military Technology.* 26, no. 12 (December 2002): 17–21.

Golawski, Artur. "Armia z przyszłoscia" [An army with a future]. *Polska Zbrojna.* 2000. www.polska-zbrojna.pl/artykul.html?id_artykul=234.

Goldgeier, James M., and Michael McFaul. *Power and Purspose: U.S. Policy toward Russia after the Cold War.* Washington, DC: Brookings Institution, 2003.

Græger, Nina, Henrik Larsen, and Hanna Ojanen. *The ESDP and the Nordic Countries, Four Variations on a Theme.* Helsinki and Berlin: Ulkopoliittinen instituutti and Institut für Europäische Politik, 2002.

Graham, Bradley. "Military Spending Sparks Warnings." *The Washington Post* March 8, 2004: A-01.

Grant, Charles, and Ulrike Guerot. "A Military Plan to Cut Europe in Two." *Financial Times,* April 16, 2003.

"Greece." *Military Technology* 28, no. 1 (January 2004): 120–23.

Grochowski, Janusz B. "Armia 2006" [Army 2006]. *Polska Zbrojna.* 2000. www .polska-zbrojna.pl/artykul.html?id_artykul=263.

Haftendorn, Helga, Robert O. Keohane, and Celeste A. Wallander, eds. *Imperfect Unions: Security Institutions over Time and Space.* Oxford: Oxford University Press, 1999.

Hampton, Mary N. "NATO, Germany, and the United States: Creating Positive Identity in Trans-Atlantia." In *The Origins of National Interests,* edited by Glenn Chafetz, Michael Spirtas, and Benjamin Frankel, 235–69. London: F. Cass, 1999.

Haukkala, Hiski. "Two Reluctant Regionalizers? The European Union and Russia in Europe's North." UPI Working Papers 32. Ulkopoliitenen instituutti, 2001.

Heikka, Henrikki. *Grand Strategies and the Northern Dimension of European Security: Four Scenarios for 2010.* Helsinki and Berlin: Ulkopoliittinen instituutti and Institut für Europäische Politik, 2003.

Heiselberg, Stine. "Pacifism or Activism: Towards a Common Strategic Culture within the European Security and Defense Policy?" IIS Working Paper no. 2. Copenhagen: Danish Institute for International Studies, 2003.

Helsingin Sanomat, February 8, 2004.

Helsingin Sanomat, June 3, 2004.

"Helsinki European Council, Presidency Conclusions." December 10–11, 1999. http://europa.eu.int/council/off/conclu/dec99/dec99_en.htm.

Heurlin, Bertel, and Mikkel Vedby Rasmussen, eds. *Challenges and Capabilities: NATO in the 21st Century.* Copenhagen: Danish Institute for International Studies, 2003.

———. *Challenges and Capabilities: NATO in the 21st Century, Supplement.* Copenhagen, Danish Institute for International Studies, 2003.

Heurlin, Bertel, Kristian Soby Kristensen, Mikkel Vedby Rasmussen, and Sten Rynning, eds. *New Roles of Military Forces, Global and Local Implications of the Revolution in Military Affairs.* Copenhagen: Danish Institute for International Studies, 2003.

Hill, Luke. "Lessons Learned Are Key to NATO Transformation." *Jane's Defence Weekly,* November 19, 2003.

Hodge, Carl Cavanagh. *Atlanticism for a New Century: The Rise, Triumph, and Decline of NATO.* Upper Saddle River, NJ: Pearson-Prentice Hall, 2005.

Hodgson, Glenn. "The Economic Cost of Terrorism." *Export Development Canada* (July 2004): www.edc.ca/docs.ereports.speeches/2004/Economics/07_04_terrorism_e.pdf.

Holdanowicz, Grzegorz. "An Uphill Task." *Jane's Defence Weekly,* September 26, 2001.

Holmström, Mikael. "Sex av tio säger nej till Nato" [Six out of ten say no to NATO]. *Svenska Dagbladet,* January 17, 2004.

Holtz-Eakin, Douglas. "Letter to Honorable Kent Conrad, Committee on the Budget." Congressional Budget Office, June 25, 2004. www.cbo.gov.

Howorth, Jolyon, and John T. S. Keeler, eds. *Defending Europe: The EU, NATO and the Quest for European Autonomy.* New York: Palgrave Macmillan, 2003.

Hughes, David. "Net-Centric War's Focus Should Be Counter-Terrorism." *Aviation Week & Space Technology* 157, no. 25 (December 16, 2002): 55.

Hughes, James. "Russia and the 'Counter-Terrorism' Campaign." *German Law Journal* 2, no. 16 (October 2001).

Huldt, Bo, Teija Tiilikainen, Tapani Vaahtoranta, and Anna Helkama-Rågård, eds. *Finnish and Swedish Security: Comparing National Policies.* Stockholm: Swedish National Defense College, 2001.

Hulsman, John C. "Cherry-Picking as the Future of the Transatlantic Alliance: The Reemergence of European Gaullism." In *The Transatlantic Relationship: Problems and Prospects,* edited by Sabina A. M. Auger, 59–66. Washington, DC: Woodrow Wilson International Center for Scholars, 2003.

"Hungary." *Military Technology* 28, no. 1 (January 2004): 147–49.

Hunter, Robert E. *The European Security and Defense Policy: NATO's Companion—Or Competitor?* California: Rand, 2002.

IMF Direction of Trade Statistics Yearbook 2000. Washington, DC: International Monetary Fund, 2000.

Institute of Strategic Stability. "Transcript of Press Conference for Russian and Foreign Media by Russian Minister of Foreign Affairs Sergey Lavrov Following Informal Meeting of the Russia-NATO Council's Foreign Ministers: Statement of Russia's Ministry of Foreign Affairs," April 5, 2004. www.iss.niiit.ru/sobdog-e/sd-168.htm.

Isidore, Chris. "Airline Woes Extend Beyond 9/11." *CNN Money* (September 20, 2003).

Iurin, Aleksandr. "The Year of the Elephant Begins in the United States." *International Affairs* 49, no. 1 (February 2003): 11–16.

Jane's Defence Weekly. "Balancing Act: Modernization Under Threat," April 11, 2001.

Jane's Defence Weekly. "Germany Cuts Budget: But Clears A400M for Take-off," December 6, 2002.

Jian, Feng. "Yearender: NATO Sharpens Edge to Confront Future Challenges." *Xinhua General News Service,* December 19, 2003.

Joenniemi, Pertti, and Jan Prawitz. *Kaliningrad: The European Amber Region.* Aldershot, UK: Ashgate, 1998.

Johnston, Karin L. "The United States, Russia, and Germany: New Alignment in a Post-Iraq World?" AICGS Policy Report #9. Johns Hopkins University: The American Institute for Contemporary Studies, 2003.

Kasekamp, Andres, ed. *The Estonian Foreign Policy Yearbook 2004.* Tallinn: The Estonian Foreign Policy Institute, 2004.

Kaufman, Stuart J. "NATO, Russia, and the Baltic States." PONARS Policy Memo No. 216. Prepared for the PONARS Policy Conference, Washington, DC. January 25, 2002.

Kauppila, Laura Eleonoora. "The Baltic Puzzle: Russia's Policy towards Estonia and Latvia, 1992–1997." Postgraduate thesis, University of Helsinki, 1999.

Kay, Sean. "What Went Wrong with NATO?" *Cambridge Review of International Affairs* 18, no. 1 (April 2005): 73–87.

Kean, Thomas H., and Lee H. Hamilton. *The 9/11 Report, The National Commission of Terrorist Attacks Upon the United States*. New York: St. Martin's Press, 2004.

Keeter, Hunter. "NATO Response Force Key to Alliance Transformation." *Defence Daily International*, May 2, 2003.

Keller, Patrick. "Germany Update." *Konrad Andenauer Stiftung* 7 (March 2003): 1–4.

Kemp, Ian. "UK Details Armed Forces Restructure." *Jane's Defence Weekly*, July 28, 2004.

Kiefer, Francine S. "Germans Move to Reassure Eastern Europe." *The Christian Science Monitor*, June 19, 1991.

Kivinen, Olli. "The Significance of the Gulf of Finland." *Helsingin Sanomat*. May 13, 2003.

Konflikty etniczne w Europie środkowej i Południowo-Wschodniej. Warsaw: Ośrodek Studiów Wschodnich, September 2002.

Kortunov, S. "Kaliningrad and Russia–Europe Partnership." *International Affairs* 49, no. 2 (April 2003): 111–32.

Kramer, Mark. "Kaliningrad Oblast, Russia, and Baltic Security." PONARS Policy Memo 10. Harvard University, October 1997. www.csis.org/ruseura/ponars/policymemos/pm_0010.pdf.

Krepinevich, Andrew F. "The Unfinished Revolution in Military Affairs." *Issues in Science and Technology* 19, no. 4 (Summer 2003): 65.

Krickus, Richard J. *Russia in NATO: Thinking about the Unthinkable*. Copenhagen: Danish Institute for International Affairs, 2002.

Kristovskis, Grits Valdis. "The Cornerstone of Latvia's Defence Policy." *NATO's Nations and Partners for Peace* 4 (2002): 128–29.

Kujat, Harald. "Beyond Istanbul." *NATO's Nations and Partners for Peace* 49, no. 1 (2004): 140–44.

Langton, Christopher, ed. *The Military Balance 2002–2003*. London: International Institute for Strategic Studies, 2002.

———. *The Military Balance 2004–2005*. London: International Institute for Strategic Studies, 2004.

Lassinantti, Gunnar. "Small States and Alliances—A Swedish Perspective." In *Small States and Alliances*, edited by Erich Reiter and Heinz Gärtner, 89–98. Heidelberg and New York: Physica-Verlag, 2001.

"Latvia." *Military Technology* 28, no. 1 (January 2004): 137–39.

Legien, Wolfgang. "Focus on the Baltic Sea Area." *Naval Forces* 24, no. 3 (2003): 68.

Leibich, André. "East Central Europe: The Unbearable Tightness of Being." Working Paper, International Security Studies at Yale University, New Haven, 1999. www.ciaonet.org/wps/lia01/.

Lejiņš, Atis. "Effects of Baltic EU Membership on Northern Europe," Conference Report–Riga: Latvian Institute of International Affairs, 2001.

Likhachev, Vassily. "Russia and the European Union." *International Affairs* 49, no. 1 (February 2003): 55–64.

Lindstrom, Gustav. "The Headline Goal." Institute for Security Studies, July 2004.

Lithuanian Defence Policy White Paper. Ministry of National Defence of the Republic of Lithuania, 2002.

"Lithuania." *Military Technology* 28, no. 1 (January 2004): 139–40.

Lok, Joris Janssen. "Germany Looks to the Future." *Jane's Defence Weekly*, August 8, 2001.

Looney, Robert. "Economic Cost to the United States Stemming from the 9/11 Attacks." *Strategic Insights* 1, no. 6 (August 2002). www.ccc.nps.navy.mil.si/aug02/homeland.asp.

Lugar, Richard G. "NATO and the Greater Middle East." Speech, 40th Munich Conference on International Security, February 7, 2004. www.europarl.eu.int/meetdocs/committees/afet/20040217NATO/Lugar.pdf.

Lugar, Richard G. "NATO Must Join War on Terrorism." United States Senate Press Releases, January 17, 2002. www.senate.gov/~lugar/011702.html.

Lynch, Dov. "Russia's Strategic Partnership with Europe." *The Washington Quarterly* 27, no. 2 (Spring 2004): 99–118.

Mahnken, Thomas G. "War in the Information Age." *Joint Force Quarterly* (Winter 1995–1996): 39–43.

Mahoney, Christine. "Allied Command Transformation—A New Way Ahead, A New Day Ahead for NATO." Allied Command Transformation Public Information Office, June 19, 2003. www.act. nato.int/multimedia/articles/2003/0961903 establish.htm.

Marshal, Will, and Peter Rudolf. "Debate: Should the Middle East Be NATO's New Central Front?" *NATO Review* (Spring 2004).

Martinsen, Kåre Dahl. *Asset or Burden: Poland as NATO's New Eastern Frontier.* Oslo: Institutt for forsvarsstudier (IFS), 2001.

McDermott, Roger. "Historic Russia-NATO Maneuvers." *Eurasia Daily Monitor* 1, no. 70, August 10, 2004.

McDermott, Roger N. "Putin's Military Priorities: Modernizing the Armed Forces." In *Russian Military Reform 1992–2002,* edited by Anne C. Aldis and Roger N. McDermott, 259–277. Portland, OR: Frank Cass Publishers, 2003. www.jamestown.org/publications_details.php?volume_id=401&issue_id=3043&article _id=2368385.

Mearsheimer, John J. "The False Promise of International Institutions." *International Security* 19, no. 3 (Winter 1994–1995): 5–49.

Menon, Anand. "From Crisis to Catharsis: ESDP after Iraq." *International Affairs* 80, no. 4 (2004): 631–48.

Michel, Leo G. "NATO Decisionmaking: Au Revoir to the Consensus Rule?" *Strategic Forum* 202 (August 2003): 1–8.

Michta, Andrew A., ed. *America's New Allies: Poland, Hungary and the Czech Republic in NATO.* Seattle and London: University of Washington Press, 1999.

Michta, Andrew A. "Central Europe and the Baltic Littoral in NATO." *Orbis* 48, no. 3 (Summer 2004): 409–21.

Mihkelson, Marko. "Baltic-Russian Relations in Light of Expanding NATO and EU." *Demokratizatsiya* 11, no. 2 (Spring 2003): 270.

Millen, LTC Raymond A. *Reconfiguring the American Military Presence in Europe.* Strategic Studies Institute, February 2004.

Ministerstwo Obrony Narodowej. *Podstawowe informacje o budżecie MON na 2004 rok.* Warsaw: Ministerstwo Obrony Narodowej, Departament Budżetowy, 2004.

Ministry of Defence. "Another £3. 7 Billion for Britain's Defence." Press release no: 100/04, July 12, 2004. http://news.mod.uk/news_press_notices.asp?date =1089586800000&show=day.

Ministry of Defence of Finland. *Finnish Security and Defence Policy 2001.* Report by the Government to Parliament on June 13, 2001. www.defmin.fi/index.phtml/ chapter_id/2575/lang/3/menu_id/356/show/all#2575.

Ministry of Defence, Republic of Latvia. *Latvian Republic Defence Budget for Year 2002.* R?ga; Author, 2002. www.mod.gov.lv/index.php?pid=1220.

————. *Report of the Minister of Defense to the Parliament (Saeima) on State Defense Policy and Armed Forces Development for the Year 2001.* Rīga, Latvia: Ministry of Defence, 2001. www.mod.gov.lv/index.php?pid=13203.

Missiroli, Antonio. "Central Europe between the EU and NATO," *Survival* 46, no. 4 (Winter 2004–05): 121–36.

Missiroli, Antonio, ed. *Bigger EU, Wider CFSP, Stronger ESDP? The View from Central Europe.* Paris: The European Union Institute for Security Studies, Occasional Papers #34, April 2002.

Mite, Valentinas. "Russia/EU: New Travel Rules Begin for Kaliningrad, with Only Minor Hitches Reported." *Radio Free Europe/Radio Liberty*, July 1, 2003. www.globalsecurity.org/military/library/news/2003/07/mil-030701-rfel-155533 .htm.

Moniac, Rüdiger. "German Defence Row." *Jane's Defence Weekly,* September 20, 2000.

————. "Leaked German Report on Armed Forces Sparks Policy Row," *Jane's Defence Weekly,* May 17, 2000.

"A More Ambitious and Expanded Framework for the Mediterranean Dialogue." Istanbul Summit, NATO Policy Document. July 9, 2004. www.nato.int/docu/comm/ 2004/06-istanbul/docu-meddial.htm.

Morrow, James. "Arms Versus Allies: Trade-offs in the Search for Security." *International Organization* 4 (1993): 207–33.

Morrow, James D. "Alliances and Asymmetry: An Alternative to the Capability Aggregation Model of Alliances." *American Journal of Political Science* 35, no. 4 (November 1991): 904–33.

Moshes, Arkady. "EU Enlargement in the Baltic Sea Region and Russia: Obvious Problems, Unclear Solutions." PONARS Policy Memo 171. Washington, DC: Institute of Europe, Center for Strategic & International Studies, 2000.

Möttölä, Kari. "Finland, the European Union and NATO—Implications for Security and Defense." In *Small States and Alliances,* edited by Erich Reiter and Heinz Gärtner, 113–124. Heidelberg and New York: Physica-Verlag, 2001.

Mróz, Marcin. "*Program przebudowy i modernizacji technicznej sił zbrojnych RP w latach 2001–2006" w świetle informacji Rady Ministrów o jego realizacji w 2001 roku.* Warszawa: Kancelarja Sejmu, Biuro Studiów i Ekspertyz, Raport Nr. 197, 2001.

Myers, Steven Lee. "Putin Says New Missile Systems Will Give Russia a Nuclear Edge." *The New York Times,* international section, November 18, 2004.

National Security Council. *The National Strategy of the United States of America.* Washington, DC: U.S. Government Printing Office, 2002. www.whitehouse.gov.nsc/nss.pdf.

NATO and International Organisations Department, Ministry of Defence, Republic of Estonia. *Estonia and International Peace Operations.* Tallinn: NATO and International Organisations Department, Ministry of Defence, Republic of Estonia, 2002.

NATO. "Istanbul Cooperation Initiative." Istanbul Summit, NATO Policy Document. July 9, 2004. www.nato.int/docu/comm/2004/06-istanbul/docu-cooperation.htm.

———. "Istanbul Summit Communiqué." News release, June 28, 2004. www.nato.int/docu/pr/2004/p04-096e.htm.

———. "NATO Elevates Mediterranean Dialogue to a Genuine Partnership, Launches Istanbul Cooperation Initiative." *NATO Update,* July 9, 2004. www.nato.int/docu/update/2004/06-june/e0629d.htm.

———. *The Prague Summit and NATO's Transformation.* Brussels: NATO Public Diplomacy Division, 2003.

Nevala, Seppo. "Speech of the Chief of the Finnish Security Police." In *The Finnish Security Police Annual Report 2003, English Summary.* Helsinki: The Finnish Security Police, 2003. www.poliisi.fi/poliisi/supo/home.nsf/pages/446DF80B096E4FB5C2256BE90041835.

New York Times. "German Town Wary of U.S. Troop Pullout," August 17, 2004.

Nitschke, Stefan. "Network-Centric Warfare—The European Initiatives." *Military Technology* 28, no. 3 (March 2004): 18–24.

"NATO Response Force." *NATO Briefing.* NATO Public Policy Diplomacy Division, Brussels, May 2004.

"Norway." *Military Technology* 28, no. 1 (January 2004): 147–49.

"Norway's Armed Forces, A Summary of CHOD Norway's Defence Study 2003." MFU, Oslo, Norway.

Norwegian Defense Department. *The Further Modernisation of the Norwegian Armed Forces 2005–2008: Proposition to Parliament No. 42 (2003–2004), Short Version.* Oslo: Norwegian Defense Department, 2004.

Norwegian Ministry of Defence. *The Long Term Defence Plan for 2002–2005.* Oslo, Norway: Forsvarsdepartementet. http://odin.dep.no/fd/english/doc/handbooks/010011-120018/dok-bn.html.

———. *Norway's Future Defense, The Implementation Proposition: A Short Version of Government Proposition No. 55, 2001–2002.* Oslo: Norwegian Ministry of Defence, 2002.

———. *Norwegian Defence 2004.* Oslo, Norway: Forsvarsdepartmentet, 2004. http://odin.dep.no/fd/english/doc/handbooks/010011-120064/dok-bn.html.

———. *Restructuring Year 2003: A Shortened Version of the Norwegian Defence Budget for 2003 (Proposal No. 1 (2002-2003) to the Storting).* Oslo, Norway: Forsvarsdepartementet. http://odin.dep.no/filarkiv/163605/Kort_eng_251002.pdf.

Nygren, Bertil. "NATO Expansion: Implications for Russian Policy Toward Ukraine and Belarus." Paper for the Salzburg meeting June 2004.

Oakley, Robin. "Prague Summit to Transform NATO." November 20, 2002. www.cnn.com.

Obwód kaliningradzki w kontekście rozszerzenia Unii Europejskiej [The Kaliningrad District in the context of the enlargement of the European Union]. Warsaw: Ośrodek Studiów Wschodnich, 2001.

Olderg, Ingmar. "Kaliningrad: Problems and Prospects." In *Kaliningrad: The European Amber Region*, edited by Pertti Joenniemi and Jan Prawitz, 1–32. Aldershot, UK: Ashgate Publishing, 1998.

Osgood, Robert E. *Alliances and American Foreign Policy*. Baltimore: Johns Hopkins Press, 1968.

Osgood, Robert Endicott. *The Nature of Alliances* (unpublished paper; 196?, Hoover Library, Stanford University).

Owens, William A. "The American Revolution in Military Affairs." *Joint Force Quarterly* (Winter 1995–1996): 37–38.

Owens, William A. "The Once and Future Revolution in Military Affairs." *Joint Force Quarterly* 31 (Summer 2002): 55–61.

Parry, Emyr Jones. "After Prague: Relations Between NATO and the EU." *RUSI Journal* 148, no. 1 (February 2003): 46–50.

Patten, Chris. "Common Foreign & Security Policy." http://europa. eu.int/comm/external_relations/cfsp/doc/concl_21-09_01.htm.

Pavlov, Nikolai. "Russia and Europe: Pros and Cons." *International Affairs* 49, no. 6 (2003): 110.

Pedersen, Klaus Carsten. "Kaliningrad: Armed Forces and Mission." In *Kaliningrad: The European Amber Region*, edited by Pertti Joenniemi and Jan Prawitz, 107–117. Aldershot, UK: Ashgate Publishing, 1998.

Pełczyńska-Nałęcz, Katarzyna. *Siedem mitów na temat Kaliningradu* [Seven myths on the subject of Kaliningrad]. Warsaw: Ośrodek Studiów Wschodnich, 2002.

Pełczyńska-Nałęcz, Katarzyna. *Poszerzona Unia Europejska wobec wschodniego sąsiedztwa: problemy i rozwiązania* [The European Union and its neighborhood to the east: problems and solutions]. Warsaw: Ośrodek Studiów Wschodnich, 2003.

Polacy o możliwości pojednania z Niemcami i Ukrainą [The Poles on the prospects of reconciliation with Germany and Ukraine]. Komunikat #2154, June 18, 1999. Warsaw: CBOS [Center for Public Opinion Research], 1999.

"Poland." *Military Technology* 28, no. 1 (January 2004): 149–54.

Polska Agencja Prasowa PAP. "Poland, Denmark and Germany Sign Military Accord," News release, September 5, 1998.

———. "Kwaśniewski on Ukrainian Elections." News release, November 8, 2004.

———. "USA: Pomoc wojskowa dla Polski będzie rozważona w budżecie na 2006 r" [USA: Military assistance to Poland will be considered in the 2006 budget]. News release, March 3, 2005.

"Polsko-niemiecka wymiana dokumentów" [Polish-German exchange of documents]. June 19, 1997.

Polska Zbrojna. "Polska i RFN podpisały traktat o potwierdzeniu istniejącej między nimi granicy." [Poland and the FRG signed a treaty confirming their current border]. November 15, 1990.

Powell, Colin L. "Opening Remarks." Speech, National Commission on Terrorist Attacks Upon the United States, U.S. Department of State Office of the Spokesman, Washington, DC, March 23, 2004.

Pravda. "Federation Council Speaker: Baltic Fleet Is Weighty Argument in Russia's Negotiations With Europe Over EU and NATO," September 9, 2002. http:// english.pravda.ru/politics/2002/09/09/36204.html.

Prime Minister's Office. *Finnish Security and Defence Policy 2004.* Government Report 6/2004. Helsinki: Prime Minister's Office: Publications Office, 2004.

Prime Minister's Office. *Finnish Security and Defence Policy 2004.* Government Report 6/2004. Helsinki: Prime Minister's Office, Publications 18/2004, 2004.

Prizel, Ilya. "Putin's Russia, the Berlin Republic, and East Central Europe: A New Symbiosis?" *Orbis* 46 (Fall 2002): 685–99.

Proceedings: NATO Enlargement After 2002: Opportunities and Challenges. Washington, DC: National Defense University, 2001.

Puhl, Detlef. "Germany and the US—What's Next? Repair the Damage?" *American Institute for Contemporary German Studies,* n.d. www.aicgs.org/c/puhl. shtml.

Quinlan, Michael. *European Defense Cooperation: Asset or Threat to NATO?* Washington, DC: Woodrow Wilson Center, 2001.

Rasmussen, Mikkel Vedby. *A New Kind of War: Strategic Culture and the War on Terrorism.* Copenhagen: Danish Institute for International Studies, 2003.

Read, David W. "The Revolution in Military Affairs: NATO's Need for a Niche Capability Strategy." *Canadian Military Journal* (Autumn 2000): 15–24.

Reiter, Dan. *Crucible of Beliefs: Learning, Alliances, and World Wars.* Ithaca and London: Cornell University Press, 1996.

Reiter, Erich and Heinz Gärtner, eds. *Small States and Alliances.* Heidelberg: Physica-Verlag, 2001.

Republic of Poland. Ustawa z 11 września 2003 r. o służbie wojskowej żołnierzy zawodowych [The Law of 11 September 2003 on the service of professional soldiers]. *Dziennik Ustaw,* nr. 179, poz. 1750.

Reuters. "Russia Proposes NATO-Compatible Peacekeeping Force," February 10, 2005.

Rhodes, Edward. "Rethinking the Nature of Security: The U.S. Northern Europe Initiative." Center for Global Security and Democracy: Rutgers University, 2002. www.copri.dk/publications/Wp/WP%202002/9-2002.doc.

Rieker, Pernille. "From Nordic Balance to Europeanisation? The EU and the Changing Security Identities of the Nordic States." Norwegian Institute of International Affairs (NUPI). Paper prepared for "Fagkonferanse for NFE," August 28–29, 2003, Kristiansand.

Robertson, George. "NATO & Mediterranean Security: Practical Steps Towards Partnership." *RUSI Journal* (August 2003): 50–52.

Rothschild, Joseph. *Return to Diversity: A Political History of East Central Europe Since World War II.* 2nd ed. New York & Oxford: Oxford University Press, 1993.

Rothstein, Robert L. *Alliances and Small Powers.* New York and London: Columbia University Press, 1968.

Royal Danish Embassy. "Denmark: A Staunch Supporter of the U.S. in Iraq." News release, November 13, 2003. www.denmarkemb.org/news/Pressemeddelelse131103 .html.

Rühle, Michael. "Continental Drift? Reflections on the Transatlantic Security Relationship." American Council on Germany, Occasional Paper #4, 2003.

———. "NATO After Prague: Learning the Lessons of 9/11." *Parameters* (Summer 2003): 89–97.

Rumsfeld, Donald H. "The Power of the Alliance." *NATO's Nations and Partners for Peace* 49, no. 1 (2004): 48–53.

"Russian Federation." *Military Technology* 28, no. 1 (January 2004): 198–203.

Rzeczpospolita. "Amerykańskie skrzydła dla Polski" [American wings for Poland]. December 28, 2002.

———. "Gonimy sojuszników" [Catching up with the Allies]. January 31, 2001.

———. "To był dobry rok" [This was a good year]. December 31, 2004.

———. "Wielka Europa Joschki Fischera" [Great Europe of Joschka Fischer]. November 14, 2003.

Saarinen, Timo K. "Developing Logistics Systems for the Finnish Defence Forces." *Army Logistician* 35, no. 1 (January/February 2003): 16–21.

Sangiovanni, Mette Eilstrup. "Why a Common Security and Defence Policy Is Bad for Europe." *Survival* 45, no. 2 (Winter 2003): 193–206.

Saunders, Paul J. "The U.S. and Russia After Iraq." *Policy Review* 119 (June 2003).

Schröder, Gerhard. "Mut zum Frieden und Mut zur Veränderung" [The courage for peace and the courage to change]. *Regierungserklärung von Bundeskanzler Gerhard Schröder am 14. März 2003 vor dem Deutschen Bundestag.* Berlin: Willy-Brandt-Haus Materialien, 2003.

Schroeder, Paul. "Historical Reality vs. Neo-realist Theory." *International Security* 19 (1994): 108–48.

Schwede, Igor. "The Baltic Naval Squadron Baltron." *NATO's Nations and Partners for Peace* 49, no. 1 (2004): 125–26.

Schweller, Randall L. "Bandwagoning for Profit: Bringing the Revisionist State Back In." *International Security* 19, no. 1 (Summer 2004): 72–107.

Scott, William B., and David Hughes. "Nascent Net-Centric War Gains Pentagon Toehold." *Aviation Week & Space Technology* 158, no. 4 (January 27, 2003): 50.

"A Secure Europe in a Better World." Brussels: EN, December 2003.

Shamberg, Vladimir. "Russia in Search of Its Place in the Post–Cold War World." Special edition, *Airpower Journal* (1995). www.airpower.maxwell.af.mil/airchronichles/ apj/shamberg/html.

Sharm el-Sheikh Fact-Finding Committee. *The Mitchell Plan, April 30, 2001.* The Avalon Project at Yale Law School. www.yale.edu/lawweb/avalon/mideast/mitchell _plan.htm.

Shen, Dingli. "Can Alliances Combat Contemporary Threats?" *Washington Quarterly* 27, no. 2 (Spring 2004): 165–79.

Siverson, Randolph, and Emmons, Juliann. "Democratic Political Systems and Alliance Choices in the Twentieth Century." *Journal of Conflict Resolution* 35 (June 1991): 285–306.

Smorodinskaya, Natalia. "Kaliningrad's Economic Growth Problem." In *Russia and the European Union*, edited by Oksana Antonenko and Karen Pinnick, 263–276. London: Routledge, 2004.

Snyder, Glenn H. "Alliance Theory: A Neorealist First Cut." *Journal of International Affairs* 44 (1990): 103–23.

Snyder, Glenn H. *Alliance Politics*. Ithaca and London: Cornell University Press, 1997.

Sørensen, Catharina. *"Ever closer union" and Contemporary Exclusionary Populism: The Emergence of European Integration and Immigration as Today's Critical Issues for Denmark*. Copenhagen: Danish Institute for International Studies, 2003.

Splidsboel-Hansen, Flemming. "Russia's Relations with the European Union: A Constructivist Cut." *International Politics* 39, no. 4 (December 2002): 399–421.

Starr, Harvey, and Siverson, Randolph. "Alliances and Geopolitics." *Political Geography Quarterly* 9 (1990): 232–48.

Stent, Angela, and Lilia Shevtosova. "America, Russia and Europe: A Realignment?" *Survival* 44, no. 4 (November 2002): 121–34.

Stent, Angela. "A New Security Agenda for U.S.-German-Russian Relations: Interim Report." AICGS Policy Report #3, Johns Hopkins University: The American Institute for Contemporary Studies 2002. www.aicgs.org/publications/PDF/policyreport3.pdf.

Stosunek do mniejszości narodowych [Attitude to national minorities]. Komunikat #2192, September 9, 1999. Warsaw: CBOS, 1999.

Struck, Peter. "Future of NATO." Speech, 40th Munich Conference on Security Policy, February 7, 2004. Berlin: Bundesministerium der Verteidigung, 2004. www.europarl.eu.int/meetdocs/committees/afet/20040217NATO/Struck.pdf.

———. "Weisung für die Weiterentwicklung der Bundeswehr" [Directive for the future development of the Bundeswehr]. Berlin: Bundesministerium der Verteidigung, October 2003.

Struck, Peter. *Defence Policy Guidelines*. Berlin: Bundesministerium der Verteidigung, May 21, 2003.

Study on NATO Enlargement. NATO Basic Texts, NATO On-line Library, *September 1995*. www.nato.int/docu/basictxt/enl-9501.htm.

Stütz, Göran. *Opinion 2003*. Stockholm: Styrelsen för psykologiskt försvar [Psychological Defense Agency], 2003. www.psycdef. se.

Supreme Headquarters Allied Powers Europe. "The NATO Response Force—NRF." News release, February 12, 2004. www.nato.int/shape/issues/shape_nrf/nrf_intro.htm.

"Sweden." *Military Technology* 28, no. 1 (January 2004): 172–75.

Swedish Defence Commission. *Defence for a New Time* (Ds 2004:30). Stockholm: Swedish Ministry of Defence, June 1, 2004, www.sweden.gov.se/sb/d/3980/a/24674.

Swedish Defence Commission. *Gränsöverskridande sårbarhet—gemensam säkerhet* [Cross-Border Vulnerability—Common Security], No. Ds 2001:14. Stockholm: Försvarsberedningen, 2001. www.regeringen.se/sb/d/108/a/1336.

———. *Säkrare grannskap—osäker värld* Sammanfattning [Summary, *A More Secure Neighbourhood—Insecure World*]. No. Ds 2003:8. Stockholm: Försvarsberedningen, 2003.

———. *Swedish Security Policy in the Light of International Change.* Stockholm: Swedish Ministry of Defence, 1998.

———. *Our Future Defence: The Focus of Swedish Defence Policy 2005–2007.* Government Bill 2004/05:5. Stockholm: Regeringskansliet [Government Offices of Sweden], 2004.

———. Summary of *Defence for a New Time,* June 16, 2004. Stockholm, Sweden: Ministry of Defence. www.sweden.gov.se/sb/d/2219/fromdepartment/2060.

Szabo, Stephen F., and Mary N. Hampton. "Reinventing the German Military." AICGS Policy Report. The John Hopkins University: American Institute for Contemporary German Studies, 2003.

Sztandar Młodych. "Wielkie zmiany" [Great changes]. April 19–21, 1991.

Tagesspiegel. "Es gibt eine friendliche Alternative" [There is a peaceful alternative]. February 14, 2003.

Telewizja Polska. *Linia specjalna.* TVP broadcast, December 18, 2004.

Teltschik, Horst, ed. *Euro-Atlantic Partnership and Global Challenges in the New Century.* Berlin: Berlin Verlag Anrno Spitz, 2001.

Tenet, George. *The Tenet Plan: Israeli-Palestinian Ceasefire and Security Plan, Proposed by CIA Director George Tenet, June 13, 2001.* The Avalon Project at Yale Law School. www.yale.edu/lawweb/avalon/mideast/mid023.htm.

Tertrais, Bruno. "The Changing Nature of Military Alliances." *Washington Quarterly* 27, no. 2 (Spring 2004): 135–50.

The Irish Times. "Pro–US Stance Pays Off for 'New Europe,'" February 12, 2005.

Theil, Stefan. "What Really Divides New from Old Europe Is Not Iraq and America but the Fear of a Resurgent Russia on Their Doorstep. That Means the Two Are Both Closer Than People Think—and Much Further Apart." *Newsweek International Edition* December 29, 2003: 46.

Thiele, Ralph. "Bundeswehr Transformation: Towards a 21st Century Transatlantic Partnership." Remarks at roundtable co-hosted by the Heritage Foundation and the Konrad Adenauer Foundation. Washington, DC, October 31, 2003.

Toremans, Guy. "Baltic Navies—Eager to Join NATO." *Naval Forces* 23, no. 3 (2002): 25–32.

"Unpopularity Begins at Home: Denmark." *The Economist,* March 20, 2004.

U.S. Department of Defense. "Fiscal 2005 Department of Defense Budget Release." News release, February 2, 2004. www.defenselink.mil/releases/2004/nr20040202 0301.html.

———. *Department of Defense Budget Fiscal Years 2004/2005.* Washington, DC: Office of the Undersecretary of Defense (Comptroller), 2003. www.dod.gov.

U.S. Department of Homeland Security. "Fiscal Year 2005 Overview." *Homeland Security Budget in Brief Fiscal Year 2005.* Washington, DC: Author, 2002. www.dhs.gov.

Ukraina wobec Rosji: stosunki dwustronne i ich uwarunkowania [Ukraine and Russia: Bilateral Relations and Their Determinants]. Warsaw: Ośrodek Studiów Wschodnich, 2001. www.osw.waw.pl/pub/prace/nr3/01.htm.

Ulrich, Marybeth Peterson. "Achieving Military Capabilities in the 'New NATO': Assessing Central Europe's New Allies." Paper prepared for the CeeISA/ISA International Convention, Salzburg, Austria, July 6–8, 2004.

Umbach, Frank. "The Future of the ESDP." Contribution to the conference "New Europe, Old Europe and the New Transatlantic Agenda," Warsaw, September 6, 2003.

United States Mission to NATO. "Denmark." Allied Contributions to the War Against Terrorism. http://nato.usmission.gov/Contributions/Denmark.htm.

Vallance, Andrew. "Military Matters: A Radically New Command Structure for NATO." *NATO Review* (Autumn 2003).

Valpolini, Paolo. "Country Briefing: Italy—At Full Stretch." *Jane's Defence Weekly*, July 7, 2004.

Vershbow, Alexander. "NATO and Russia: Redefining Relations for the 21st Century." *Hampton Roads International Security Quarterly* (March 30, 2002): 21–26.

Vinokurov, Evgeny. "Economic Prospects for Kaliningrad Between the EU Enlargement and Russia's Integration Into the World Economy." Working document 201. Brussels: Centre for European Policy Studies, 2004. http://shop.ceps.be/Book Detail.php?item_id=1123.

———. "Kaliningrad's Borders and Transit to Mainland Russia: Practicalities and Remaining Bottlenecks." Brussels: Centre for European Policy Studies, 2005. www.ceps.be/Article.php?article_id=264&.

Voskopoulos, George. "U.S. Terrorism, International Security, and Leadership: Toward a U.S.-EU-Russia Security Triangle." *Demokratizatsiya* 11, no. 2 (Spring 2003): 165.

Walker, Martin. "The New Russia Takes Shape." *Europe* 417 (June 2002): 6–9.

Wallander, Celeste A. "U.S. Policy on Russia and NATO." Prepared for the "Integrating Russia Into Europe" project, Brussels conference, July 8–9, 2002.

Wallander, Celeste A. "US-Relations: Between Realism and Reality." *Current History* 102, no. 666 (October 2003): 307.

Wallander, Celeste A., and Robert O. Keohane. "An Institutional Approach to Alliance Theory." Working Paper 95-2, The Center for International Affairs, Harvard University, Cambridge, MA, 1995.

Walt, Stephen M. *The Origin of Alliances*. Ithaca and London: Cornell University Press, 1987.

Ward, Adam, and James Hackett, eds. "The Quadrennial Defense Review, Competing Demands." *IISS Strategic Comments* 11, no. 1 (February 2005).

———. "US Defence Spending, Battling with Budgets." *IISS Strategic Comments* 11, no. 1 (February 2005).

Weitsman, Patricia A. *Dangerous Alliances: Proponents of Peace, Weapons of War*. Stanford, CA: Stanford University Press, 2004.

Weizsaecker, Richard V., Peter-Heinrich Carstens, Theo Sommer, Christian Bernzen, Christoph Bertram, Ignatz Bubis, Eckhard Cordes, et al. *Gemeinsame Sicherheit und Zukunft der Bundeswehr. Bericht der Kommission an die Bundesregierung* [Common security and the future of the Bundeswehr. The Commission's Report to the Federal Government]. Berlin: Kommission Gemeinsame Sicherheit und Zukunft der Bundeswehr, 2000.

White House. "President Bush Speaks to Faculty and Students of Warsaw University." News release, Warsaw, Poland, June 15, 2001. www.whitehouse.gov/news/releases/2001/06/20010615-1.html.

Więcej niż sąsiedztwo: Rozszerzona Unia Europejska i Ukraina—nowe relacje. Rekomendacje [More Than Neighbors: The Enlarged European Union and Ukraine. Recommendations]. Warsaw: Fundacja im. Stefana Batorego, 2004. www.batory.org.pl/doc/rekomendacje_pl.pdf

Wielgo, Marek. "Inwestycje NATO w Polsce nabierają rozmachu." *Gazeta Wyborcza.* December 1, 2004.

Williams, Michael C., and Iver B. Neumann. "From Alliance to Security Community: NATO, Russia and the Power of Identity." *Millennium: Journal of International Studies* 29, no. 2 (2000): 357–87.

WISE-Paris. "Plutonium Proliferation and Non-Proliferation [*sic*]: Sweden—Plutonium Investigation No. 14/15." WISE-Paris. www.wise-paris.org/index.html?/english/ournewsletter/14_15/page3.html&/english/frame/menu.html&/english/frame/band.html.

Index

About the Author

Andrew A. Michta is the Mertie W. Buckman Distinguished Professor of International Studies at Rhodes College in Tennessee (on leave 2005–2008), currently teaching as professor of national security studies at the George C. Marshall European Center for Security Studies in Germany. He holds a Ph.D. in International Relations from the Paul H. Nitze School of Advanced International Studies at Johns Hopkins University (1987).

He is the author of *The Soldier-Citizen: The Politics of the Polish Army after Communism* (1997), *The Government and Politics of Postcommunist Europe* (1994), *East Central Europe after the Warsaw Pact: Security Dilemmas in the 1990s* (1992), and *Red Eagle: The Army in Polish Politics, 1944–1988* (1990). He is coeditor and coauthor with Ilya Prizel of *Polish Foreign Policy Reconsidered: Challenges of Independence* (1995) and *Postcommunist Eastern Europe: Crisis and Reform* (1992). He has also written articles and book chapters on European security and politics, postcommunist transition, civil-military relations, and NATO. His most recent book is *America's New Allies: Poland, Hungary and the Czech Republic in NATO* (1999).